HOW TO M▪▪ PER YEAR INCOME A▪ THE W▭RLD

The Passive Income Guide to Wealth and Financial Freedom

Features 14 Proven Passive Income Strategies and How to Use Them to Make $100K Per Year

By Chase Andrews

DISCLAIMER :

Published by
CAC Publishing LLC
ISBN 978-1-948489-04-1 eBook
ISBN 978-0-9987140-3-5 paperback

If you're interested in learning more about me, passive income, and how to take back your life, make sure to check out my site at www.thepassiveincomemachine.com see you there!

If you enjoy learning about passive income in this book, a review would be MUCH appreciated! Leaving reviews is the best way to help your fellow readers differentiate good books from terrible ones so make sure to help out your fellow readers and passive income enthusiasts!

Make sure to check out my series titled 'Your Path to Success.' The first book in the series is titled Fail Your Way to Success and it highlights how great achievers view success and how they used failure to their benefit every single time. With failure they not only elevated themselves, they took humanity to greater heights with them.

Contents

PREFACE

This book is about freedom. It is my personal mission to free as many people from the rat race as I possibly can. When I reached out to the experts you will read about in this book, at least half of them responded back with, "My connection may be a little spotty, I'm currently on an island in the Philippines." Or "I am on a year-long road trip across the USA and Central America with my family." Do you know why they are able to live that lifestyle? Because they have learned how to generate passive income!

"The trouble with the rat race is that even if you win, you're still a rat." – Lily Tomlin

They have beat "the system" and now live the way that THEY want to live. No one tells them what to do, they don't have to ask their boss to take time off, and they aren't tied down to a city they don't like just because their job is there. What's even better, I interviewed 12 of these passive income experts and they all agreed to share their secrets right here in this book! All that is required from you is ACTION.

"Many a false step was made by standing still." – Fortune Cookie

You wouldn't be reading this book if you didn't want something to change. The problem is that most people want change, but they never *change* anything. How can your life change if you don't do anything to change it? Break the mold and change your life. Put the following strategies into action and see what happens.

"If you do what you've always done, you'll be what you've always been." – Matt Hasselbeck, former NFL Quarterback

INTRODUCTION

What is Passive Income

Passive income – making tons of money without doing a single thing! Right?

That seems to be the classic definition that so many eager entrepreneurs believe, and it doesn't help that the Internal Revenue Service (IRS) defines passive income as "Income that can only be generated by a passive activity."[1] Thanks for all of the info, IRS.

I know what you're thinking: "I do passive activities all the time! As a matter of fact, I'm sitting on my couch right now!" Just imagine how great passive income is the way most people think about it. It's Sunday, you're sitting on your couch eating potato chips, watching the big game. Meanwhile, people are throwing money through your windows; all you have to do is duck so you don't get hit in the head with all that cash!

Unfortunately, the IRS states that there are only two sources for passive income:

1. A rental activity; or,

2. A business in which the taxpayer does not materially participate.

Bummer. I don't see sitting on the couch listed anywhere! No organization in the world knows how to put a damper on your dreams quite like the IRS, am I right? The second point in their definition I

---

[1]

https://www.irs.gov/businesses/small-businesses-self-employed/passive-activity-loss-atg-chapter-3-passive-income find particularly interesting. "A business in which the taxpayer does not materially participate." This actually continues to etch into our brains that passive income is so easy, you don't even have to participate. "Man, if I can just buy the right product, it will do everything for me and I will only need to cash the checks!"

So what exactly is passive income? The simplest definition of passive income is doing something once, and getting paid for that "something" over and over again — like writing a book. You spend all of your time upfront writing the book itself, but once the book is finished, you collect the checks every time it sells, with no further action required.

What that definition doesn't tell you is that a lot of the time, the "doing something once" part can take weeks, months, years, and even decades in some cases. Also, more often than not, it actually does take some ongoing work.

What is *passive* income?
Passive income is when you do the work ONCE...
... and you get paid over and over again, month after month.

However, I do believe that there is a second definition of passive income. To me, passive income represents freedom. Of course, everyone wants to do something once and get paid for it over and over, but not all passive income streams I mention in this book work that way. In fact, there really aren't many truly passive streams of income out there. Passive income is more about a lifestyle. It's having freedom to do what you want to do, and work when you want to work.

Why You Need Passive Income NOW

Millions of people are spending their entire lives working in a "normal" job that they hate. The worst part is they do this just to survive. If they get fired or have an emergency, then what? Living paycheck to paycheck doesn't leave any wiggle room for the unexpected.

We have not been educated about wealth creation, about money, about passive income, about financial freedom. Why? Our educational system is based on the 19th century Prussian model – it is designed to create foot soldiers and factory workers who will blindly follow the "rules" and not strive to step outside of what is considered "normal." This model has taught us to get a "good job" and work hard for our money.

That is why millions of people trade their time for money. They do their "job" for a month or two weeks, and then get paid for that work. If they want to get paid again, they have to go back to work. They continue to repeat this process their entire lives without ever learning the secrets of wealth creation or passive income.

Earned income
Earned income is linear.

You work for 30 days...
You get paid...   You spend your money...
Then you have to work for another 30 days...
And on, and on, and on, for 40+ years.

But what happens when your company tells you they are letting you go? More importantly, what happens to your family? I hate to break the news to you, but the big corporation you work for doesn't give a crap about you! They pretend to care when the company is making

3

money, but what is the first thing they do when the numbers go the other way? When is the last time you got a nice raise? What about a bonus?

I know you aren't worried about that though. You've been stashing a good amount of your paycheck away into your retirement account, or maybe you have a nice pension waiting for you. But can you really rely on that to help you survive? If you get laid off or want to retire early, you will take a massive hit in fees and penalties for trying to get YOUR money.

What about social security, pension funds, or other government-sponsored programs? Can you count on the government to fund your retirement? Here is what Simon Black, editor of the "Sovereign Man" newsletter, has to say about that...

"Governments around the world are in a similar situation to Madoff right now with their own public sector Ponzi schemes. Faced with failed auctions, declining demand, and rising yields, politicians are having to resort to desperate measures."

"This is a truly despicable act and amounts to theft, plain and simple. All over Europe, governments are sponsoring new marketing campaigns suggesting that it's people's patriotic duty to buy government debt."

"The UK, which is rapidly reaching banana republic debt status itself, has unveiled a plan to issue roughly $50 billion in infrastructure bonds. Given Britain's already colossal debt level, private investors aren't exactly diving in head first to loan the government even more money."

"Undeterred, British Chancellor George Osborne plans to 'highly encourage' UK pension funds to mop up about 60% of the total amount."

"'We have got to make sure that British savings in things like pension funds are employed here and British taxpayers' money is well used,' he said. In other words, 'we are going to make sure that British people buy our junk, one way or another.'"

"The last year has seen numerous pension funds around the world, from the United States to Argentina to Hungary, be raided for the sake of keeping these Ponzi schemes going. The UK is already lining up to be the next. It's one of the last

acts of a truly desperate government to begin directing public and private savings into their Ponzi schemes."

Simon Black, SovereignMan.com

Furthermore, whether you know it or not, a lot of the workforce is in jeopardy of losing their jobs to robots or machines. The imminent IT takeover has been in the works for decades, and the pace is accelerating. Experts believe the rapid development of technology will reach its peak in the next 50-100 years. Mankind has never advanced further in technology than where we are now. Perhaps 75% of the jobs will be gone in 50 years.

No existing or future job, without exception, is safe. Computers are being programmed to think exactly like humans. Remember Watson, the IBM computer that competed on Jeopardy against former winners? He smoked them and took home the first place prize of a million bucks. Watson was programmed to think like a human and it consistently outperformed the human opponents on the signaling device.

Robots or computer-assisted humans produce goods and services more cheaply and efficiently than humans. In our capitalist system, robots will win out over their human counterparts as the companies who decide to use emerging technology dominate the marketplace with bigger profits and accelerated growth. The world's capital is moving by leaps and bounds to automation and away from investing in human labor, simply because it produces better ROI.

What is the solution? You must work for passive income NOW, before a disaster happens to you. Stop exchanging your time for money. The longer you continue to do that, the longer you stay in the rat race. You have to change the way you think about money and rewire your brain. You need to stop buying things to impress people you don't like with money you don't have.

"Annual income twenty pounds, annual expenditure nineteen six, result happiness. Annual income twenty pounds, annual expenditure twenty pound ought and six, result misery." — Charles Dickens, David Copperfield

Want to be wealthy? Spend less than you make and WISELY invest the difference.

"With every dollar that comes into your hand, you have a CHOICE. If you're smart, you'll use that dollar to buy an income-generating ASSET! Once a dollar goes into your asset column, it becomes your employee. The best thing about money is that it works for you 24 hours a day… for generations!" —Robert Kiyosaki

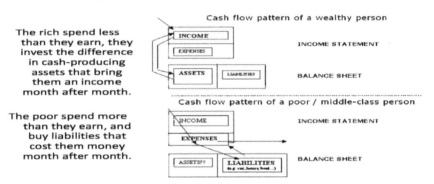

The rich spend less than they earn, they invest the difference in cash-producing assets that bring them an income month after month.

The poor spend more than they earn, and buy liabilities that cost them money month after month.

Passive Income For the Lifestyle You Want

Today, passive income entrepreneurs are setting up home-based businesses all over the world, wherever they want, and they are bringing in $3,000 to $100,000 per month in passive income. These people work much less than the people with "normal" jobs, and they make much more. They can get up and travel whenever they want. The income streams they have set up continue to make money for them whether they are working or not.

"A desk is a dangerous place from which to view the world." – John Le Carre

No more working for an unhappy boss whose main goal is to make everyone else's lives as miserable as theirs. No more coworkers who constantly nag and complain about every little thing. No more sitting in traffic for hours on end commuting to a job you hate, surrounded by people you don't like, working for a company you could care less about. No more being forced to live in a city you hate only because your "job" is there.

Imagine being able to CHOOSE where you want to live. No more having the taxman take your money if you don't want them to. You can just move to a country that doesn't have income tax. Yes, places actually exist with no tax. For example, Seychelles, an archipelago of 115 islands located in the Indian Ocean, has NO TAX. You can actually live on a beautiful island in the middle of the ocean and keep ALL of your money. Doesn't that sound crazy?

"Your time is limited, so don't waste it living someone else's life." – Steve Jobs

Every single strategy that I mention in this book can be done from anywhere in the world. All you need is an internet connection.

The Mindset You Need to Create Passive Income

Generating wealth, being financially free, creating passive income: if you want all of these things, there is only one thing you have to do – SOLVE PEOPLE'S PROBLEMS. It really is THAT simple! Think about it: everyone in the world has a problem (most of us have way more than one, but this book doesn't have enough pages to talk about all those problems). No money, health issues, weight problems, nowhere to live, depression — the list goes on and on. Wouldn't you give someone money if they could help you with your weight loss struggle? What if someone creates a product that makes your life easier? What if someone provided housing for you? If you can create VALUE, if you can really HELP OTHERS, people will happily pay you for that service. *"Life is to make an IMPACT, it's not only to make INCOME"* — Sivaprakash Sidhu

In Mark Anastasi's book, "The Laptop Millionaire," he has a fantastic section about defining what exactly "money" is. In it, he states: *"money is nothing but the measure of the value that you create for other people. This means, of course, that money flows to the people who are providing the most amount of value."*

7

I love this definition as it rings so true. Think about some of the wealthiest people in the world. For example, Bill Gates and Paul Allen, the founders of Microsoft, have a combined net worth of over $97 BILLION dollars. The money in their bank accounts is an exact representation of how much value they have created and delivered.

Jeff Bezos, the founder of Amazon; Mark Zuckerberg, the founder of Facebook; Sam Walton, the founder of Wal-Mart; what do they all have in common (aside from being filthy rich)? They all solved millions of people's problems! From making shopping easier to creating new ways to connect with each other, it's all the same idea: helping people meet a need or solve a problem. So you want to make Bill Gates or Mark Zuckerberg money, right? From now on, I want you to stop thinking, "How can I make more money?" Instead, think, "How can I create more value for more people?" Once your mindset has shifted, you will be amazed at how money continually flows your way based on the value you create.

The only thing that this book cannot do for you is take action. One of the most common questions I hear is, "If this is really so great, why isn't everyone else doing it?" The answer is human nature. People are scared of change. They're afraid to step outside of their comfort zone. ANYONE can implement just about every one of these strategies. The key is: when will you start?

"Whenever you find yourself on the side of the majority, it is time to pause and reflect." – Mark Twain

Remember, if you aren't happy with your life, you can change it. But if you never take action, nothing will change. Try something from this book TODAY. If you wait, you may never start and you'll stay right where you are forever. You NEED this, and you need it NOW.

"Tomorrow becomes never." – Timothy Ferriss

CHAPTER   1:
Amazon Kindle Direct Publishing

Amazon is the largest online retailer in the world. Amazon Kindle is the most popular eReader on the market today, by far. Combine the two, and it makes for a perfect place for online business seekers who want to create passive income by selling books on Amazon Kindle.

Finding a Niche

Browse around the Kindle store and check out the best sellers. This is a list of the bestselling books that are currently on Kindle. This is extremely valuable information, because it shows you the hot markets where people are already spending their money.

Another way to get a sense of successful topics is to check out the categories. If you go to Amazon > Shop by Department > Books & Audible > Kindle Books, you will see a full list of categories on the left hand side of the page. Click on "Nonfiction" to sort out the fiction books.

This is where you click around and start brainstorming ideas for topics. You should try to find 12 or more topics that interest you. Even more specifically, look at the keywords of the popular books and write those down. In the screenshot above, some examples of popular keywords would be "Millionaire" or "War" or "Money." In a top 20 list, you could expand even more. There was a book about metabolism, one about great salads, and one about changing your habits.

You aren't getting to your niche yet. At this point, you are only finding your broad target market.

Market Research

A common mistake that new entrepreneurs make is creating products that they *think* will sell. They invest hours in researching the topic, creating the product, and posting it for sale only to find out it doesn't sell at all.

You can publish a New York Times bestseller quality book that has a great topic, a great cover, and great content, but if there is no market for it, it won't make you much money. Find the market first. Create the product second.

Finding the Best Keywords

Your first step in the market research process is to find the exact keyword or phrase that people are searching for on Amazon. Always make sure you are doing this search in the Kindle store, not the larger Amazon marketplace. Otherwise, you are researching physical products instead of books, and that will throw you way off.

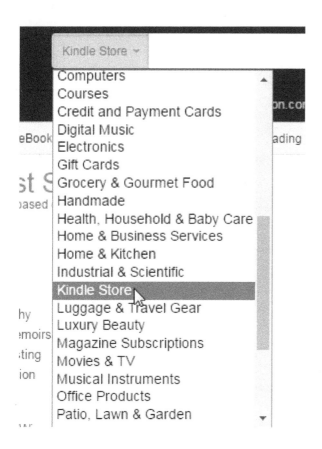

Once you have Kindle Store selected, you will want to type in your keyword in the search bar. Amazon will automatically provide suggestions of popular searches that people are typing in. This is extremely valuable information to find out what the hot topics are and where the demand is.

In our keyword research above, we identified "Millionaire" as a potential topic. Let's type that in the search bar and see what comes up.

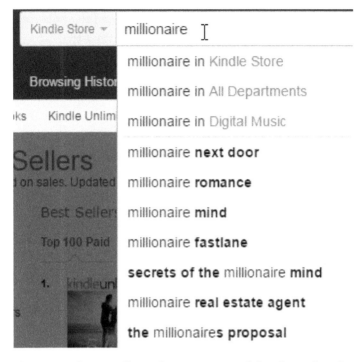

You now have a list of seven potential sub-topics that you know people are actively looking up for you to base your book on.

Let's say you move forward and use "millionaire fastlane" as your keyword. If you type that in, you'll see there are 57 results in the Kindle Store for those keywords. The more books, the more competition, and the more difficult it will be to rank at the top of this list. The less competition, the easier it will be to get to the top — but don't get discouraged by thousands of results. After all, Amazon suggested those keywords because they're popular and common.

You can analyze the search results more carefully for a better idea of your future competition. Remember, people who search for something typically choose between the top 3-5 results, so that's where you want to be. Analyze those top results. If they are weak listings, with few or unfavorable reviews, you can easily outrank them and take over the position.

The most important thing to worry about here is the strength and quality of those first few Kindle books for your chosen keywords, so don't focus on the whole list so much as those first five slots.

Find What Sells

You can check to see if those top 3-5 search results products are actually selling. For this step of the research, you want to focus on books that are similarly priced to the book you want to sell and with a reasonable number of reviews. We will stick to a range of $2.99 - $3.99 for this and avoid the books that are selling for $12 and have hundreds of reviews. The publishers of those books likely have means that you as an individual don't.

Using our keyword "millionaire fastlane" from earlier, I chose a book priced at $2.99 with just a few reviews. To find out if this book is making any money, scroll down to the Product Details section.

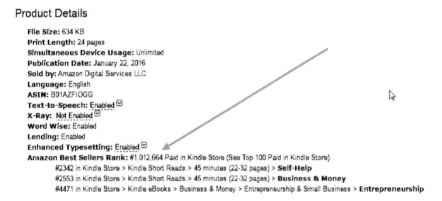

Product Details

File Size: 634 KB
Print Length: 24 pages
Simultaneous Device Usage: Unlimited
Publication Date: January 22, 2016
Sold by: Amazon Digital Services LLC
Language: English
ASIN: B01AZFIOGG
Text-to-Speech: Enabled
X-Ray: Not Enabled
Word Wise: Enabled
Lending: Enabled
Enhanced Typesetting: Enabled
Amazon Best Sellers Rank: #1,012,664 Paid in Kindle Store (See Top 100 Paid in Kindle Store)
  #2342 in Kindle Store > Kindle Short Reads > 45 minutes (22-32 pages) > Self-Help
  #2553 in Kindle Store > Kindle Short Reads > 45 minutes (22-32 pages) > **Business & Money**
  #4471 in Kindle Store > Kindle eBooks > Business & Money > Entrepreneurship & Small Business > **Entrepreneurship**

Every book that is in the Kindle Store is ranked by how well it sells. This one, for example, is ranked #1,012,664. It's best to find books that are ranked #100,000 or better. Based on the leading industry research, if a book is ranked in the top 100K, selling at $2.99, and with a 70% royalty, it is probably making around $50 per month. If that book is ranked 10,000-50,000, it could very well be making hundreds of dollars per month at the same price.

With one of the top results ranking only #1,012,664, it may not be a worthwhile pursuit to publish a book with these keywords. To be sure, you can investigate a few others from the similarly priced top results. If those aren't selling well either, it may be best to try your next keyword.

Let's try another search phrase, like "high protein low carb diet." When I start typing the keywords, Amazon suggests a number of popular searches, including the keyword we're investigating. This is a very positive sign.

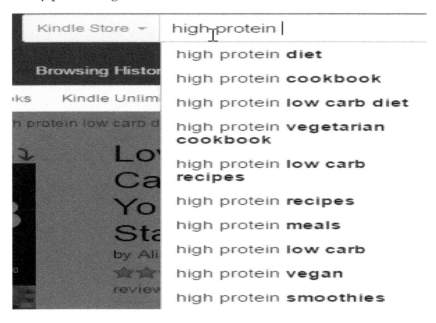

I typed in "high protein low carb diet," and up popped 388 search results. Let's examine similarly priced and reviewed books and see if this topic has potential.

The first book that came up has product details as follows:

Look inside ↓

READ ON
ANY DEVICE
› Get free Kindle app

Low Carb: The Ultimate Low Carb High Protein Diet To Lose Your Weight Quickly without Starving Kindle Edition

by Alisha Abbott ▾ (Author), John McKerihan (Editor)

☆☆☆☆☆ ▾   32 customer reviews

▸ See all formats and editions

Kindle
$0.00 kindleunlimited

This title and over 1 million more available with Kindle Unlimited
$3.45 to buy

Welcome to the Low-Carb Recipes Cookbook, What is the Lo Carb?

The low-carb, high-protein diet is a simple, healthy way to los weight and feel better. Enjoy the best health of your life, and

Product Details

File Size: 2464 KB
Print Length: 111 pages
Simultaneous Device Usage: Unlimited
Publisher: Aston Publisher (October 26, 2015)
Publication Date: October 26, 2015
Sold by: Amazon Digital Services LLC
Language: English
ASIN: B0177ZN1M4
Text-to-Speech: Enabled ☑
X-Ray: Not Enabled ☑
Word Wise: Enabled
Lending: Enabled
Enhanced Typesetting: Enabled ☑
Amazon Best Sellers Rank: #86,986 Paid in Kindle Store (See Top 100 Paid in Kindle Store)
   #25 in Books > Cookbooks, Food & Wine > Special Diet > **High Protein**
   #95 in Kindle Store > Kindle eBooks > Health, Fitness & Dieting > Diets & Weight Loss >
   #97 in Kindle Store > Kindle eBooks > Cookbooks, Food & Wine > Special Diet > **Low C**

Ranked #86,986. That fits our criteria, so things are looking good. This book probably makes well over $100 per month. Don't base your results on one book — continue examining the next three or four to get a solid picture of the market for this niche.

The second book also produced good results.

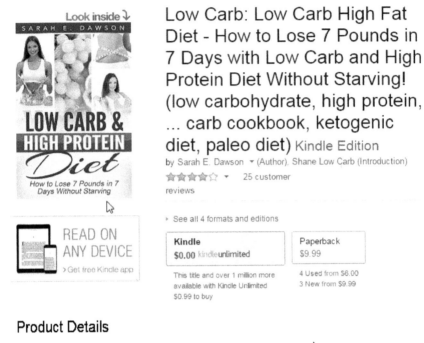

Product Details

File Size: 2574 KB
Print Length: 64 pages
Simultaneous Device Usage: Unlimited
Publication Date: May 2, 2015
Sold by: Amazon Digital Services LLC
Language: English
ASIN: B00X2CGMV4
Text-to-Speech: Enabled
X-Ray: Not Enabled
Word Wise: Enabled
Lending: Enabled
Enhanced Typesetting: Enabled
Amazon Best Sellers Rank: #55,783 Paid in Kindle Store (See Top 100 Paid in Kindle Store)
　　　#1 in Kindle Store > Kindle eBooks > Nonfiction > Sports > **Rodeos**
　　　#3 in Books > Sports & Outdoors > **Rodeos**
　　　#12 in Books > Cookbooks, Food & Wine > Special Diet > **High Protein**

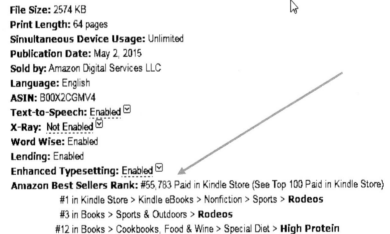

This one comes in ranked even better at #55,783.

On to search result #3:

High Protein Low Carb Diet: Lose Weight Effortlessly & Permanently Kindle Edition

by Jennifer Jenkins ▾ (Author)

⭐⭐⭐⭐☆ ▾   70 customer reviews

▸ See all 5 formats and editions

Kindle	Paperback
$0.00 kindleunlimited	$12.99
This title and over 1 million more available with Kindle Unlimited $2.99 to buy	10 Used from $11.04 20 New from $8.79

If you're trying to lose weight for the first time (or for long time now), this may be the most important book you'll ever read...

Unlike other diet books, the *High Protein Low Carb Diet* g

Product Details

File Size: 2046 KB
Print Length: 44 pages
Publication Date: January 26, 2014
Sold by: Amazon Digital Services LLC
Language: English
ASIN: B009S9VRS8
Text-to-Speech: Enabled ☑
X-Ray: Enabled ☑
Word Wise: Enabled
Lending: Enabled
Enhanced Typesetting: Enabled ☑
Amazon Best Sellers Rank: #284,482 Paid in Kindle Store (See Top 100 Paid in Kindle Store)
    #89 in Books > Cookbooks, Food & Wine > Special Diet > **High Protein**
    #280 in Kindle Store > Kindle eBooks > Cookbooks, Food & Wine > Special Diet > **Low Carb**
    #455 in Kindle Store > Kindle Short Reads > 90 minutes (44-64 pages) > **Cookbooks, Food & Wine**

This one comes in ranked outside of our criteria at #284,482, so it's probably not making too much money. We can settle for books ranked outside of 100,000 if they are priced slightly higher than our target price of $2.99. If a book is ranked 150,000, but is priced at $3.99, that book can still be making over $100 per month.

We got two out of three that were in our criteria. This could be a good market to pursue, but don't be afraid to keep searching for a keyword that comes back positive for the first five results.

You should analyze the search results for other factors too. Check out the number of pages, the number of five star reviews, etc. If a top-selling book with your keyword has 300 pages, it will be hard for you to create a cost-effective alternative with a 50-page book.

If the #3 book has 24 reviews, but they only ranked at three stars, you know you can do better than them — so go for it! Create a better cover, come up with a catchier title, get more great reviews, add more pages, etc. These are all things you can do to make your book stand out.

Creating a Great Title and Cover That Sells

Your book will sell based on a few major factors: title, cover, and reviews. When people are looking for a book to read, they likely have no clue who you are and they have no idea if your book is crap or gold. They base their decision solely on whether your book stands out from the rest.

Title

You must have your primary keyword in the title of your book. Amazon will even rank your book better based on how early the keyword appears in the title. Keyword optimization, much like Search Engine Optimization, is the most important factor in your titles. Put your keywords at the beginning.

You can add related keywords to your title as well. That way, you will rank higher for all similar keywords in addition to your main keywords. This strategy can increase your sales dramatically. For example, if your primary keyword is "high protein low carb diet," put that as your first five words, but then add something related. A great title for this topic would be, "High Protein Low Carb Diet: Simple High Protein Low Carb Diet Recipes to Help You Lose Weight." Now your book will rank for your primary keyword, and it will also rank for a secondary keyword like "high protein low carb diet recipes" or "low carb diet recipes." Don't be afraid to make your title longer to be more descriptive.

Cover

Most of us are not very creative, so don't try to be. To create a high quality cover that sells, get a professional to do it on fiverr.com or upwork.com. It shouldn't cost you more than $5 to $10. Just type in "Kindle cover" on either site and you'll get a whole list of people who will create a cover for you.

Always filter these results based on ratings. Some of the top-rated people will charge more, but it's better safe than sorry. If they have thousands of great ratings, they do great work.

The designer will likely request the information they need from you once you place an order, but feel free to send them the details so they can get started right away. You will want to send them the title, the subtitle, and an image to start with, if you have one. If you don't have an image, they can do that for you, too.

Books with images tend to sell better than ones without. An eye-catching image will help your book stand out from the crowd, more so than a cover that just uses text. If you have a preference about fonts or colors, make sure to tell your designer upfront which fonts and colors to use for the cover.

Book Creation

People these days have extremely short attention spans. Shorter books tend to sell better on Kindle because the majority of people don't want to spend too long reading a book. For Kindle books, think less is more — even 50 pages is fine. This will also limit your cost of production, which is key since we don't know how well any particular book will sell.

The quality of your book will not be determined by the length. There are plenty of books in the Kindle Store with over 300 pages that don't sell at all and are full of fluff. Instead of length, focus on value: make sure your content is useful and actionable. The length doesn't matter.

If you want to write your own Kindle books, you won't be able to produce very much, and you'll find yourself struggling to generate enough content to generate a worthwhile income. A better option is to have a ghostwriter do the writing for you.

Again, you can use upwork.com or fiverr.com for this as well. Make sure that you are hiring native English speakers to write your books. This is key. It's nothing against other languages, but if English isn't the writer's first language, it will come across in the writing.

You can give the writers as little or as much detail as you want. You could just provide them the title and subtitle and tell them to have at it, or you can provide them the research articles to use as the basis. Either way will work, as long as you choose a good writer based on ratings.

You can even go as far as providing a book template for your writers to follow. Once you get a few books under your belt, you will find this makes things much easier because you'll know exactly what to expect in the finished product.

Before you publish your book, you will want to have it formatted and proofread. Sometimes the ghostwriter will offer to do this for you, but it is probably best to get fresh eyes on it. Throw out another few bucks and have someone else format it and proofread it for you. Think about how many errors you missed in your own school papers growing up. With your Kindle books, you're not just getting graded — you're (hopefully) getting paid, so hiring a proofreader or editor is a valuable investment.

Publishing on Kindle

The first step to publishing your book on Kindle is to create an account. Head on over to kdp.amazon.com and sign up for your account. If you have purchased items from Amazon before, you will just need to log in.

You will need to complete all required information that Amazon asks for. The details that the site requires for opening a new account can vary depending on where you're located, so we won't cover that here.

Once you finish creating your account and have everything set up, head to your "Bookshelf." This is basically a dashboard, just like every other e-commerce site — Amazon just used a clever name. Once you navigate to your Bookshelf, click the "Add New Title" button. This will bring you to a page requesting detailed information.

You will have the option of enrolling your book in the KDP Select program. This is a program for Amazon Prime members where they pay a fee and are able to "borrow" a book for free each month. You still make money when someone borrows your book, so don't worry about losing profits. Enrolling in KDP Select will help your book rank higher in the results, and it allows you to promote your book for up to five days every 90 days for free through the program. Just keep in mind that you won't be able to publish your book anywhere else for those 90 days.

Book Details

Step one: enter the title of your book. You can leave the Edition and Publisher blank. You may want to select "This book is part of series," as this will allow you to create a series title in which you can add additional keywords to help in search results.

The description of your book is extremely important. People will make the decision to buy or not based almost entirely on the description. If the description is interesting, they buy it. If it's boring, uninspiring and bland, they don't. You're allowed 4,000 characters in KDP to write your description, and I suggest you use as much of it as possible.

Also make sure to include as many keywords and related keywords as possible in your description. This can boost your rankings even further.

Pen Name

The next section is for adding contributors. It is highly suggested that you use a pen name for this, unless you wrote the book yourself. Don't feel weird about this — it's extremely common among writers. Even Mark Twain, J.K. Rowling, and George Orwell were all pen names.

Publishing Rights

Now, onward to verify your publishing rights. In this case, since the book is 100% original and you own all content, you want to select "This is not a public domain work and I hold the necessary publishing rights."

Categories

Kindle lets you select up to two categories for your book. You should think carefully about selecting the categories best suited to your particular book. Your goal here is being able to rank within the top 100 of that particular category. If you have selected a very competitive category, you can always come back and change it if you aren't getting the desired results.

You also add in your "Search Keywords." You are allowed to add seven keywords, and you want to use the keywords from your title or series title, subtitle, as well as important words used in your description.

Uploading The Cover and Book

Click on the "Browse for Image" button and select the cover that you had created using fiverr.com or upwork.com. You'll have to make sure it's in .jpg format. If not, you can always go back to your designer and have them send the cover in .jpg format.

Next, you'll need to upload your book. You'll see an "Uploading Your Book File" section which will ask if you want to enable digital rights management or not. If you select "do not enable," others will be able to share your book. This can lead customers to other books

22

you have for sale, so it can be helpful — but it's not necessary, so feel free to select whichever option you'd like.

Then, you will see "Browse for book" option. This is where you select your actual book. It will need to be an .epub file. Once it's uploaded, you can preview it and verify it looks right. After that, click "Save and Continue" to move on.

Publishing Territories

After you upload your book and hit Save and Continue, you'll see that it asks to verify your publishing territories. Always select "Worldwide rights – all territories" as you want your book to be able to sell all over the world.

Royalties

In the "Choose Your Royalty" section, you will have two options: 35% royalty and 70% royalty. KDP will pay 35% royalty if your book is being sold from $0.99 - $2.98. For the 70% royalty, you must sell your book from $2.99 - $9.99.

You obviously want to get the 70% royalty for your books, but we are going to price our books at $0.99 to start so that we can build up reviews and get some sales. Once we have some great reviews, then we'll raise the price up to at least $2.99 and potentially higher if the book is selling really well.

Click on the 35% Royalty option and type in the price of $0.99. You should also check the boxes for all the other Amazon platforms so that your book is available to as many customers as possible.

Further towards the bottom, you will see "Allow lending for this book." This will allow people to share your book with family and friends, which is good for us because we want to get it out in front of as many eyes as we can.

Posting Your Book

Lastly, click the final check box to confirm that you have all the rights and that you agree to the KDP Terms and Conditions. It's a good idea to read the Terms and Conditions to make sure you're complying with their rules.

There you go! You'll get a message that your book is being published and will be online shortly. You'll also get an email from KDP once the book is up for sale. Well done!

Your Book is Published, Now What?

Now that your book is published and available for sale on Amazon, you should head over to the Kindle store yourself and see where your book is currently listed when you do a search for your keywords. It won't be near the top at this point, so you may have to dig a few pages deep to find it.

You'll want to take note of which page it shows up on during this first search so that you can see the improvements once you start marketing and getting some sales. You'll also want to note your current Amazon bestsellers ranking, which you will find in the same product details section that you used when doing your research.

It is also very important to find your ASIN (Amazon Standard Identification Number). This can be found in your product details section as well.

Product Details

File Size: 2464 KB
Print Length: 111 pages
Simultaneous Device Usage: Unlimited
Publisher: Aston Publisher (October 26, 2015)
Publication Date: October 26, 2015
Sold by: Amazon Digital Services LLC
Language: English
ASIN: B0177ZN1M4
Text-to-Speech: Enabled ☑
X-Ray: Not Enabled ☑
Word Wise: Enabled
Lending: Enabled
Enhanced Typesetting: Enabled ☑
Amazon Best Sellers Rank: #131,020 Paid in Kindle Store (See Top 100 Paid in Kindle Store)
    #39 in Books > Cookbooks, Food & Wine > Special Diet > **High Protein**
    #147 in Kindle Store > Kindle eBooks > Cookbooks, Food & Wine > Special Diet > **Low Carb**
    #156 in Kindle Store > Kindle eBooks > Health, Fitness & Dieting > Diets & Weight Loss > Diets > **Low Fat**

You should also check your listing and verify that everything looks the way you want it to. Check the title, the cover, the description, etc. If you need to make any updates, head back to your account and make the changes. The book will be updated within 24 hours.

Then get the link to your book. The link for the book of the product details image above is as follows:

https://www.amazon.com/Low-Carb-Ultimate-Protein-Starving-ebook/dp/**B0177ZN1M4**/ref=pd_sim_351_2?ie=UTF8&pd_rd_i=B0177ZN1M4&pd_rd_r=1TF9KR9D3VDVEPC9VJSS&pd_rd_w=YOvjk&pd_rd_wg=ojpl0&psc=1&refRID=1TF9KR9D3VDVEPC9VJSS

You only need the link up to your ASIN number, which is highlighted in the URL above. For this book, the link for you to use in marketing efforts will be https://www.amazon.com/Low-Carb-Ultimate-Protein-Starving-ebook/dp/B0177ZN1M4

Getting Reviews

Reviews are arguably the most important selling factor for your book. If your listing has no reviews, no one will buy it.

Types of Reviews

There are two types of reviews on Amazon:

- Amazon Verified Reviews

- Unverified Reviews

Amazon verified reviews are when someone purchases your book from Amazon and then leaves a review. You can find these in the Reviews section of any listing. They will have orange text in the review that says "Amazon Verified Purchase." Positive, verified reviews help your book rank higher than a larger number of unverified reviews.

Unverified reviews are when a person didn't purchase the book, but still left a review.

Number of Reviews

There is no magic number of reviews that you need to be successful. It all depends on your competition. It could be 15, 25, 35, or more. Check out your competition and see how many reviews the more successful books with your keywords have, and make that your goal.

How to Get Reviews

Organically: You can always just sit back and wait for people who buy your book to leave reviews. The biggest problem with this is that only 1 in 1,000 people actually post a review on a book they purchase.

Friends/Family: You can ask your friends or family to buy your book and then leave an honest review. You can even send the book to them as a gift by using the "Send as Gift" button on your book's listing. You have to make sure their reviews meet Amazon's review guidelines, so make sure you check that out.

Facebook/Social Media: Find a group on Facebook that might be interested in your book. If your book is about a low carb diet, find a group about that, or similar groups about weight loss or eating well. Then create a post for that group, offering to give the book for free to members who are interested in it. Interested members will message you; you can send it to them, then follow up a few days later by asking for an honest review.

Set Up a Free Promotion on Amazon: Once you start getting a few reviews using the strategies above, you can set up a free promotion by going to your KDP bookshelf and clicking "Promote and Advertise." You will have an option to use a "Free Book Promotion," which means that your book will be available for up to five days for free. Make the start date at least seven days from the current date when you set it up. Tip: Before you set up your free promotion, change the price of your book from $0.99 to $2.99. This will give your book more perceived value when it's free, and will likely lead to more downloads.

All of the reviews you get don't have to be 5 stars. It makes your listing look more natural if you have 4-star, or even 3-star, reviews mixed in. The goal is to make sure your overall rating is at least at 4 stars.

Improving Your Ranking

Besides getting reviews, there are a few other strategies you can implement to improve your ranking in the Amazon search results.

Amazon Wish List: On your book's listing, under the "Give as a Gift" link, you will see an option to "Add to Wish List." When your book is added to someone's wish list, it tells Amazon that people are interested in this book and that it is popular. The more people that add your book to their wish list, the higher your rankings. People typically use this wish list around the holidays to show friends or family members products that they want, or as a way to bookmark items for purchase later.

Making $100,000 Per Year With Kindle

You've got your books published. They are getting reviews, ranking higher and higher, and you're getting some sales. Congrats!

While generating $100/per month from one book may sound great to a lot of folks, generating $1,000/month sounds much better. Generating $10,000/month from Amazon Kindle alone sounds even better! So how can we get there?

Let's say you only want to publish Kindle books and don't want any backend sales funnel. Great! That will make this all the more passive once you get your reviews and ranking up. Based on the target we set earlier in this chapter of having an Amazon Bestsellers Rank of #100,000 or better, and having our book priced at $2.99, we can reasonably expect each book that we publish that meets that criteria to generate $100/month.

With that formula, we would need to get 100 books published on Kindle that meet the minimum criteria in order to reach our six figure goal. Sound like too many? Remember, you aren't writing these books — you are hiring people on upwork.com to do it for you. That's what makes this strategy so effective: it's very easy to get a lot of books published in a very short period of time.

Maybe you don't want to publish 100 separate books. That's fine, too. Keep reading.

Don't Want to Publish 100 Books?

I know what you're thinking, publishing 100 separate books sounds very daunting and you don't think it's feasible. Well guess what? You don't have to publish 100 Kindle books to get to the $100,000 per year goal! Wait, what? I literally just said that a few paragraphs ago, was I lying to you?

Well, actually no. If you want to make $100,000 per year with Kindle ONLY, then yes, you will probably have to publish close to 100 eBooks, but there is a much better and more feasible approach. Woohoo! (reader wipes sweat from their forehead from getting so nervous about 100 books).

The secret is to transform those Kindle eBooks into paperback books.

You may be thinking that paperback books seem too official and you have no experience doing that so this isn't for you, but it's actually WAY easier than you think.

I want to give you a little peek into my own publishing business that generates over $100,000 per year. I currently make DOUBLE the royalties from my paperback books than I do my Kindle versions. As of this writing, I'm around $6,000 per month in paperback royalties and $3,000 per month in Kindle royalties (with plans to nearly double in the next 6-12 months!).

So, using those real-life statistics, the 100-book thing is no longer the measuring stick. Let's do some math; if it was going to take us 100 Kindle books to get to $100,000, but we turned each Kindle eBook into a paperback book, now how many books do we need to publish?

100 Kindles = $100,000 ($100/month each).

If we publish a paperback version with each Kindle version, then using my own real-life ratios of approximately 2 to 1, we should be making around $300 per book per month ($100 from Kindle, $200 from paperback). $300 per month is $3,600 per year. $100,000/$3,600 = 27.78. WHOA!

So now, instead of having to publish 100 separate Kindle eBooks, we only have to publish 28 Kindle eBooks and create a paperback version from each one of those. Does 28 books sound a little more reasonable??

These stats don't even factor in Audiobooks, which are EXTREMELY popular these days. As of writing, my audiobook royalties are 1/3 of my Kindle royalties, so roughly $1,000 per month. I won't do the math, but the number of books has dropped even more now. Are you getting excited yet!?

I won't get into the full details of transforming your eBooks to paperbacks here, but check out my blog www.thepassiveincomemachine.com as I have a post that goes step-by-step of how you can turn an eBook into a paperback book without spending a dime or writing another word! Here's the direct link: http://www.thepassiveincomemachine.com/2017/06/transform-kindle-ebook-paperback-book-free/

More Ways to Get to Six-Figures

There are even more ways to reach the six figure goal with Amazon Kindle. For example, you can establish a blog or a website around the topic of your book, and then include a link to that site in your book.

When you start getting tons of sales, those readers will appreciate the value you provided in the book and want to check out your site. This is where you provide an opt-in page so they can subscribe to your list and receive any future updates on books, products, etc. related to the topic. Now, you have an email list of interested readers who have a much better chance of buying your future book or product than someone who has no idea who you are.

You can even put together a series of books related to the same topic. That way, when your first book becomes extremely popular and you've generated a nice email list, you send a quick email out to your subscribers letting them know you just published a follow-up book. Instant sales! Sales will become repeat sales and you will gain trust and authority with these readers, which will make them want to sign up to your website even more.

If you've ever heard the internet marketing saying, "It's all in the list," you now know what that means. I've heard of experts who have gotten hundreds of thousands of email subscribers to their lists. That's basically a license to print money! These guys can make millions of dollars by sending just one email. So, if you don't want to publish 100 books (or even 27 with paperbacks), just set up a website and an email list and watch what happens!

CHAPTER 2:

Amazon FBA

Amazon FBA (Fulfillment by Amazon) is one of the most fantastic opportunities out there for entrepreneurs. Their FBA program means they will literally take care of everything — warehousing, shipping, customer service, the whole works! This has opened up some great avenues for entrepreneurs interested in passive income.

Amazon is the world's largest online retailer. If you get a product listed on Amazon that means you instantly gain the trust of millions of built-in buyers!

I interviewed Amazon FBA expert, Will Tjernlund, to explain how the whole process works. Not only does this guy know the Amazon world inside and out, but he also sells millions and millions of dollars' worth of products via Amazon's FBA service. In fact, in 2014 alone, Will and his brother sold $6 million dollars of products on Amazon. Better yet, in 2015, they topped that with a whopping $10 million! That's over $800K per month!

Letting Amazon do all the "heavy lifting" work helps create a much larger business than an individual seller could ever hope to accomplish on their own. You can scale much faster and continue to run the business yourself even when your sales range into the millions of dollars. That's the beauty of the Amazon FBA service. Take advantage of it!

How to Find A Product

The key to finding a great product that will sell well is to look at what is *already* selling well. Yes, you can spend money on software that will do the work for you, but guess what? Amazon already does!

If you go to Google and type in "Amazon Top 100 Sellers," it shows you the top selling products on Amazon. You can filter by any department you want — Arts and Crafts, Electronics, Sports & Outdoors, Pet Supplies, etc.

I decided to filter by Sports & Outdoors and here's what I found:

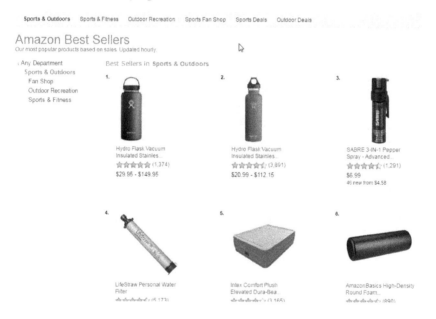

Now you instantly know that everything on that page is already selling like crazy. There's a full list of 100 potential products that you know are best sellers.

When analyzing a market for a product, Will looks at the review to revenue ratio. If there are $100,000 in total sales on the first page of the search results, and 1,000 reviews, that's $100 per review, which is a great ratio. But if there are 10,000 reviews on the first page and only

$100,000 in sales, $10 per review isn't as strong a ratio. This is a very easy, quick way to gauge where the product is in its life cycle, and whether the market is already saturated.

Will uses JungleScout.com for his analysis. Jungle Scout is a must have for all Amazon sellers, as it breaks down the competition for every search. All you have to do is type in your search, and then hit the Jungle Scout button. You'll get an entire page of data from the search results. From revenue to daily sales cost, it has every data point you will ever need to identify a strong market.

Head on over to my website www.thepassiveincomemachine.com, and use the Jungle Scout link to get a 10% discount when you sign up.

The main key to finding great products to sell is to stay niche. There is no point in competing against 1,000 other sellers of the same product. When you're doing your research, think like a buyer. If a person is searching "Power Tools," they don't know if they actually want to buy tools or not — they are just looking around. But if they search "12V Battery Powered Cordless Drill with Accessories," chances are they NEED that drill for a project and are looking to buy.

Market for "needs," not "wants." If someone is actively searching for knee scooters, the odds are that they need the scooter due to an injury. It's not a want; it's a necessity.

In the ecommerce space, it's about being creative and finding different ways to market your niches, and finding niches that haven't been developed yet. Even better, look for a niche of a niche. Avoid electronics, things with a lot of moving parts, and extremely competitive products. For example, Will mentioned there are spin mops on Amazon — that's a pretty niche marketplace in itself. But instead, go for the niche of a niche and sell the industrial spin mops, which sell for a much higher price than the regular ones.

Get lost on Amazon. Go deep into the "Items suggested for you" and don't be afraid to get obscure.

Keep An Eye Out

Finding the products to sell is one of the easiest parts of the process, according to the experts. But many individuals trying to get started say it's the hardest. They don't want to pick something with too much competition. They don't want to pick a loser. What happens to these people? They never start anything!

How does a multi-million dollar seller find products to sell? Will explained that when he first got started selling on Amazon, he was a huge UFC fan. One night, he was watching a fight when he noticed one of the fighters wearing shorts that said "Hayabusa" on them. He decided to head to his favorite site, Amazon, to check out some of Hayabusa's products.

When he searched for Hayabusa, he noticed that all of their listings were very poor quality and, being the expert, he knew he could sell more products for them. He decided to call Hayabusa directly and offer to sell their products for them. He found out that they sold to mostly smaller-sized UFC gyms across the country, and most of the sellers don't have enough cash to keep their product in inventory because they offered five different colors of gloves in five different sizes. It would cost too much in inventory for the sellers to stock everything.

Will recognized that Hayabusa needed someone with a strong cash flow to be able to stock enough inventory, and he realized he could be their main seller. He asked if the company would let him be the only authorized reseller on Amazon if he could keep all of their gear in stock. Initially, he was selling the gear in his other Amazon accounts alongside generic products. Hayabusa said they wanted a standalone Amazon account that was only selling their product.

Will created a standalone Amazon account called Fighting Factory. He also created an ecommerce site called fightingfactory.com to make sure people knew it was legit. Every month, he would buy $30,000 of inventory from Hayabusa and then sell it for $40,000 - $45,000, and it was all on repeat through FBA. Will does none of the R&D

and none of the marketing — all he has to do is reorder until the product sells out. Amazon handles all the shipping and all the returns on the customer service side of things. That's $10,000 in profit every month, without doing any of the real work!

I know what you're saying: "Yeah, but he's a pro. I could never contact real companies, why would they want me to sell?" Think about it. You're a free sales rep. Why wouldn't they let you do that? In the case of Will and Hayabusa, the company is getting one of the best Amazon consultants in the world for free. They don't pay him a dime because he buys the product from them. It's a win-win all around.

Here's a recap: Will went from a UFC fan watching TV, saw a product and contacted the company, convinced them he could sell it better, set it and forget it, and now he earns $10K/month with Amazon FBA.

Retailers

The next time you are walking around Target or Wal-Mart, take a look at the products on the shelves, particularly everything at eye level or on the ends of the aisles with nice displays. The retailers obviously want you to see those specific products. Why?

Those are the most profitable products. Those are the high margin products that the store wants you to buy so that they can make more money. Those same products can also be high margin for you, so take a look around and get some ideas to kickstart your sales.

Infomercials

We've all seen the infomercials for cool new products. The companies that make those products wouldn't pay all that money for infomercials if the products weren't making them money. There is demand for those products among people watching television, which means there is also demand on Amazon for those types of products as well.

Where To Get Your Products

Alibaba.com is the main supplier for almost all private label products you see on Amazon. Will uses them himself for every product. The key to finding great suppliers is fairly simple. You can sort the suppliers for a particular product by whether they have a gold star rating, if their facility has been independently assessed, and other criteria. You can also see how long each one has been in business so you can know they are legit.

If you're looking for yoga mats because you saw them on the top 100 in the Sports & Outdoors section, type in Yoga Mats in Alibaba and filter your suppliers.

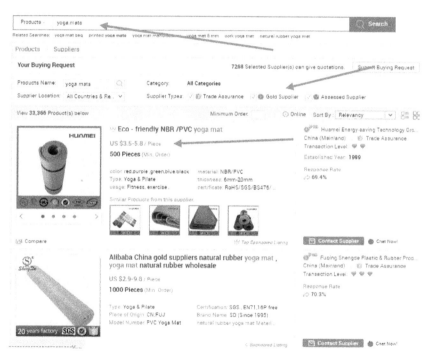

The first of the arrows is the Search Bar where I type in what I'm looking for — in this case, yoga mats. I then filter the suppliers, as you can see with the second arrow. This pulls up a list of all the suppliers who manufacture yoga mats that tells you whether the suppliers have a gold star rating, how long they've been in business, and what their prices are. In this case, the first supplier on the list can make the yoga mat for somewhere between $3.50 and $5.80.

How To Know If a Product Will Be Profitable

From our Alibaba search, we know that we can get yoga mats made for $3.50 - $5.80. You don't want to sell extremely cheap, low-end products. You should price yourself somewhere in the middle of the competition. The general rule of thumb is you want to sell products that are priced between $15 - $50. The reason we like that range is that products in it qualify as a compulsive purchase. A person probably doesn't have to get approval from their spouse to spend $25 on a yoga mat that they need for their next yoga class.

So if we price our yoga mat at $25, we know from the supplier that our shipping costs will be $4.50 per unit, and our Amazon FBA fees will be 30% of our sales price (or $7.50). Will this be a profitable product?

$25 sales price - $4.50 for shipping - $7.50 fees = $13 net profit

$13 in net profit is over 50% profit! This would be a great product to try and sell. Better yet, we haven't spent a single dime finding out if we can make money on it.

There are thousands and thousands of yoga mats sold on Amazon.com every single day. If you can take just a tiny percentage of the market share, let's say 1%, you can make a killing! If there are 5,000 yoga mats sold on Amazon every day, and you make 1% of those sales, that's 50 sales per day. At $13 net profit per sale, you would be making $650 per day, or $19,500 per month!

Our goal is only $100,000 per year, but this one example could make someone over $200,000 per year!

Private Labeling

Private labeling is simply the practice of putting a name on a generic product in order to sell it for more. If you have an unlabeled camera to sell on Amazon, maybe you sell it for $50. But put any name on it, and all of a sudden, you can sell it for $75. That's the power of private labeling and the key to any Amazon FBA business.

In another example Will provided, he mentioned the national sport of Thailand, Muay Thai. Muay Thai is a combat sport where the fighters use their knees, elbows, shins, hands, or anything else to strike their opponent. One of the UFC companies Will is interested in sells Muay Thai boxing shorts. He noticed that these simple shorts were selling like crazy for $70 a pair. $70 for nothing more than a pair of athletic shorts.

Will realized he could buy a similar product from a manufacturer, private label it, and sell it for much cheaper than the competition. This is another example of going niche. There were very few businesses selling Muay Thai boxing shorts, which is why this company could sell their shorts for $70. Will knew he could get nearly identical shorts made for a dollar in China. He bought the shorts from an Alibaba supplier, put his Fighting Factory brand on them, and sold them for $30.

Now when people search Amazon for Muay Thai shorts, they are presented with the $70 product, or Will's $30 product which is the exact same thing. That's the power of private labeling. With a $1 upfront cost per item, you can turn around and sell your product for $30 because you found a great niche and private labeled it. That's fantastic margin!

In our interview, Will also mentioned a story about how an unfortunate injury led to a business opportunity. Will's cousin slipped on a patch of ice (he's from Minnesota, so there is a lot of ice to slip on) and hurt his foot. He came to Will, knowing that he buys all sorts of products from Amazon, and asked Will to buy a knee scooter so he could move around while he healed from his injury.

Being the entrepreneur he is, Will knew this was another great niche opportunity. A lot of people hurt their legs and needed this product to get around. His cousin said the only ones he could find were close to $400. Sure enough, Will did some research on Amazon and found that the knee scooters were consistently going for $400 or more. He knew he could have something made and sell it for less.

He hopped on Alibaba and found out the same scooter could be made for $60. That's over $300 in profit margin! He started doing some research on GoDaddy.com about available domains related to this product. Using a coupon code, he bought injuredleg.com for $2.99.

Injured Leg Knee Scooters was born. He had the products manufactured, slapped the label on the box and started selling them. He sold 7 on the first day! From there, you can extrapolate the money made from this one niche product. 7 times $150 in profit per piece, times 30 days in a month — that's $31,500 in profit per month! That blows away the $100,000 target we've set in this book.

Coming up with your private label packaging and branding doesn't have to be a tough process. A lot of would-be entrepreneurs get stuck on the very first step, and they end up wasting months and months without getting anywhere. Just pick a catchy name that's available as a domain, then create a website and custom email. That way, it looks like each private label product is its own company.

Even better, you don't have to do any of that yourself. Head over to fiverr.com or upwork.com and pay someone $5 to create your logo. Pay another few bucks for a website, and there you go. In one afternoon, you can have the listing up with a professional-looking website to go along with it. It's an extremely quick way to legitimize your product. If you procrastinate, you could lose out on months of sales.

Selling Your Product

Now that you have your product and you're ready to sell, it's time to create your listing. Remember, you have a niche product that people need. Stay extremely specific in the product keywords so that your listing shows up in the top results for everyone searching for "Muay Thai shorts."

One fantastic strategy is to go to your competitors' listings and read their bad reviews, then turn those reviews around in your listing. How are you fixing the issues that other competitors are having? If you continually see a complaint that the handles are too close together on your competitor's knee scooters, make a point to mention in your description that "These handles are far apart for a perfect grip." That way, if someone is scrolling through and reads the negative review of your competitor, they'll know you have addressed that problem. That's one more sale for you, and one less for your competitor.

The key is to test the market immediately, possibly even before you have a product on hand. If the product starts selling, you know you have a winner. For these "test" sales, you can simply buy that product from someone else on Amazon and use the customer's address as the shipping address. That way, you can see what the demand is and at what price BEFORE you even buy any product yourself. If it sells well, then you know it's time to place your order. "Don't buy it first, sell it first."

After you've tested your product and you know it sells, create your listing. 98% of sellers on Amazon don't do this part correctly, but they make a ton of money anyway — so imagine how much you can make if you do it right. Think pictures, pictures, pictures. You need to have great, high-quality images of your product and lots of them. Show your product being used in everyday life.

Talk about the benefits of your product, not the features. Instead of saying your yoga mat is 2 inches thick (feature), state that it is 2 inches thick which will protect your knees and provide support and comfort to help keep you doing yoga longer so you can improve your health (benefits).

Will mentioned that his strategy for big growth was to go after certain markets and completely saturate them. He would choose certain products and private label them, but he would also contact the top five manufactures for that product and buy from them too. Then, when a customer searches for your product, you can sell them your own private label version or the one from a leading brand. Either way, they are buying from YOU.

Let's say you have a Seattle themed coffee mug. The Starbucks coffee mug sells extremely well, and a Seattle's Best Coffee mug sells too. You could create your own coffee mug with some sort of Seattle themed brand, then get in contact with Starbucks and Seattle's Best Coffee and carry those mugs too. Then if a person searches for a coffee mug from Seattle, all of the top listings lead to your products.

Most U.S. brands will sell to you wholesale if you have cash and can talk them into it. Imagine you're a salesman for a big brand and someone actually calls you wanting to buy instead of the other way around. You're doing their work for them. It's very easy to get a "yes" from these companies if you have cash and can back up your offer by placing an order. Yes, your profit margins are lower on the brand name items, but you're still making money. Hard to beat that.

Reviews

Reviews on your listing are extremely important. They are the lifeblood of your product. When you go to Amazon, do you buy anything that doesn't have reviews? No. Neither do 99% of the other people searching Amazon.

Once you get your product from the supplier and listed, give some samples away to friends and family in order to get some 5 star reviews. Due to Amazon's review guidelines, they will have to mention that they received the product for free or at a discount in exchange for their honest review, but that won't impact the 5 star rating.

Amazon ads

After you start getting some 5 star reviews, start driving more traffic to your product with Amazon Ads. When you are searching on Amazon and you see a product to the right that says "Sponsored," that is someone using Amazon ads. This is a great way to get your product on the first page of the search results and drive more sales. It does cost money, but it can be well worth it.

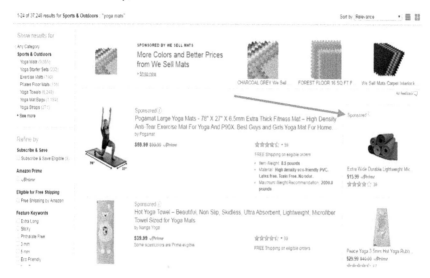

Insider Tips

Will's main advice during our interview was to go out and get products TODAY. If you continue to wait and wait, you will never get started. It doesn't matter if you lose money on the first try — just go through the process. You can buy 10 samples of small items for $10 and start selling. 99% of the questions that people ask Will can be answered by simply going through the process yourself.

Don't be scared to pull the trigger. Anyone can make money with Amazon, but most people never start. They continually second-guess themselves with questions: "What about this?" "Will this product work?" "What if it doesn't sell enough?" "What if I lose money?"

Go to Alibaba, find a $5 product that sells for $10, and go for it. Buy 10 of them, throw them up on Amazon and see what happens. Worst case scenario is you lose $50, but you've gained the knowledge of actually going through the process, which is invaluable.

CHAPTER 3

Real Estate

Real Estate is probably the most popular and most commonly implemented strategy for passive income. But be advised: investing in real estate for passive income is in no way a get-rich-quick scheme. It takes a lot of hard work and usually a lot of money upfront. It's been reported that 90% of millionaires in the world made the most of their money by investing in real estate. If that's the case, you can't argue with the results.

One of the best strategies for investing in real estate and getting passive income quickly is the BRRRR strategy that I came across on the BiggerPockets real estate forum (www.biggerpockets.com). This community of individuals interested in real estate is one of the most active sites I've found. You have everyone from newbies trying to buy their first property to millionaire real estate investors who are giving advice. If you're interested in real estate, make sure to check it out.

What is BRRRR?

BRRRR is a popular investment strategy that was made up by a BiggerPockets contributor. It stands for:

Buy

Rehab

Rent

Refinance

Repeat

To put it plainly, this strategy entails buying a rental property that needs some work, rehabbing the property to bring it to the top of the market, renting it out to great tenants, refinancing the mortgage to pull your cash back out, and then repeating this process over and over again until you get to your desired number of properties.

The site has showcased numerous individuals who now own 25+ properties thanks to this strategy. The power behind this system comes from the ability to acquire property after property without ever running out of cash to invest. At the same time, it combines the benefits of flipping a house with the obvious wealth-building characteristics of rental properties.

Now that we know what this strategy is and what it stands for, let's go over each step and break down the process even further.

Buy

Obviously, to invest in real estate you need to have a property. But this doesn't mean you can just go out and buy the first house you find. You must find a great deal. This doesn't mean a "good enough" deal — it has to be a great one.

The BRRRR strategy is basically house flipping, except instead of selling the house once the renovations are complete, you hold onto it and rent it out to great tenants. That, in turn, provides you the monthly cash flow you are looking for, assuming you got a good deal.

Here's an example. A very common real estate flipping rule is the 70% rule, which states that the most a house flipper should pay for a property is 70% of the ARV (After Repair Value), less rehab costs. ARV is what that property will be worth when all the renovations are complete. So if a house has an ARV of $100,000 and needs $15,000 worth of rehab, it should be purchased at a price of $55,000: $100,000 X 70% = $70,000

$70,000 - $15,000 = $55,000.

Do the numbers sound too good to be true? Almost all house flippers that have had success have built their entire business model on margins like these. The key is that they don't say, "I can't find properties with those numbers." They make it work with statements like, "How can I make this deal happen?"

To be successful and find good deals takes some hustle. You may have to browse Craigslist routinely, you may have to send direct mail, you may have to drive around until you see a house that looks appealing — but these are the things successful people are willing to do, and you should be too.

The caveat for your first purchase is this: it's highly unlikely that you'll be able to use a traditional lender. Most of them just aren't willing to loan money for a house that needs renovations. This still leaves a few options open: private money, cash, home equity, hard money, etc. You just have to think outside the box.

From owner-occupied investment properties, partnerships, home equity loans/lines of credit, hard money, raising private money, lease options, seller financing, to any other way to acquire property with little or no money down, they are all outlined in "The Book On Investing in Real Estate with No (and low) Money Down," by Brandon Turner (who I will mention in the next step). If you haven't read it, check it out. It will provide some fantastic knowledge on how you can complete this first step with other people's money!

Rehab

The second part of the BRRRR strategy is Rehab. This involves the renovation of your newly acquired property. Unlike house flipping, you won't be selling this property once the repairs are complete. Instead, you'll be renting it out to tenants, so you need to select materials that will give you the highest monthly rent — but maybe more importantly, you need to choose materials that can withstand tenant use for years on end.

The key to rehabbing with a BRRRR property is "tenant proofing" your place. This means using materials that are known to last a long time and won't need to be redone every few years. During the rehab, you need to keep in mind that your goal is to get the highest ARV and monthly rent possible. For example, if you find a large two bedroom home that has enough room to add a third bedroom, that's a no brainer. This can add hundreds of dollars to your monthly cash flow, not to mention increasing the value of the home and therefore providing more equity.

Brandon Turner, the VP of Growth and Communications of BiggerPockets provided one example of the rehab style to keep in mind on a BRRRR property. He was working on a BRRRR house and when the renovation crew ripped up the carpet, they discovered beautiful hardwood floors underneath. You would assume that he would save the money and just have them refinished, but instead, he added laminate on top of them for the time being. Refinishing the original hardwood floors would cost around $3 per square foot, and they would likely need to be refinished again prior to selling the property years down the road due to heavy usage by the tenants. He opted to use laminate flooring which would only cost $2 per square foot. Not only is the laminate cheaper, it will also protect the original floors underneath during tenant use. Then when he needs to sell, he can remove the laminate, refinish the floors and get top dollar for the property.

Another extremely important part of this step is to make sure you replace or correctly fix anything that needs attention. If you cut your rehab short to save a few bucks, it will cost you way more money and headache down the line when you're receiving phone calls in the middle of the night for a water heater leak. It's worth the investment now to avoid it later. Of course, you will still need to budget for maintenance and repairs, but if done right, those costs can be much lower than expected.

Rent

The third, and arguably most important in terms of passive income, part of the BRRRR process is renting your newly renovated property to GREAT tenants. If you purchased your property wisely, it's in a great location, so it shouldn't be hard to find fantastic tenants.

You can choose to hire a property manager to do this for you, or you can do it yourself. If you choose only high-class, respectful, responsible tenants, managing your property should be relatively easy. It is very wise to always have prospective tenants complete a rental application and background check. If they have terrible credit and have skipped on payments in this past, you don't want to rent to them.

Refinance

The fourth step in this process is to refinance into a nice, comfortable conventional mortgage. Earlier it was mentioned that it may be tough to get a conventional mortgage on a fixer upper, but conventional mortgages are great for investors once the house has been flipped: they usually feature extremely low interest rates, they're a stable, long-term investment, and they're typically very easy to get.

You may not need to refinance your property to get your money back. Maybe you make great money from your job and can afford to let your down payment and rehab costs stay in the property. Doing so may even help you get better monthly cash flow, and possibly even a better ROI. However, it can be beneficial to refinance and get your money back. Then you can reinvest the money and repeat the process over and over again.

Let's use the same example we used early. We found a property with an ARV of $100,000. You purchased it for $55,000 and put $15,000 into the renovations. You now have $70,000 invested in the property. Most lenders will let you refinance a property for 70% of the ARV, meaning they will do a 70% LTV loan (Loan To Value loan) on the property. Since 70% of $100,000 is $70,000 you could, in theory, get every dime you have invested in the property back.

After the refinance is complete, you should have a renovated and currently rented property that brings in a small amount of cash flow and has around 30% in equity! It's an ideal situation. The biggest part is to purchase the right property at the right price.

Repeat

Now that you've got 30% equity in a great rental property that gives you some monthly cash flow, it's time for the last step in the process. Repeat! If it worked once, why can't you replicate it?

Of course, there are limits on the number of mortgages an individual can have. The current limit is actually 10, so you could potentially repeat the process 10 times with no issues. That's 10 properties with 30% equity, all with great tenants and completely renovated — you're sitting on a gold mine! The best part is you only used your original investment for all of them as you continually got that investment back on each property.

How to Make $100,000 Per Year Using the BRRRR Strategy

Historically, real estate prices have risen, on average, 3% per year. Let's be a little more pessimistic and say we expect 2% per year for our scenario. If we bought a property today with an ARV of $150,000, only paid $75,000 for it, spent $30,000 on the renovations, rented it out, and refinanced it for $105,000, at a 2% increase per year, that same property would be worth $165,000 in five years.

Not only that, but the mortgage on that property has been paid down over the last five years and is now only at $96,000, so we also have

$69,000 in equity. If you want to sell the property, you can expect it will need some paint and other minor fixes, not to mention paying the real estate agent's commissions plus closing costs. The $69,000 in equity is, realistically, more like $50,000 in profit.

Therefore, in order to make six figures using the BRRRR strategy, you only need to buy two properties each year, and then, starting in year five, begin selling two properties each year. As long as you make the numbers work, you should never have more than 10 properties. After only five short years, you will be making $100,000 per year by only purchasing two properties per year and selling two properties per year.

That's the power of this strategy. It may seem like a lot of "what-ifs," but if you stick to the numbers, it can be extremely powerful for getting you to the six figure target and building serious wealth. Speaking of sticking to the numbers, BiggerPockets also has some fantastic tools to help you analyze deals quickly and efficiently. Again, this site is one of the most valuable sites I've come across when it comes to real estate. It even convinced me to get my first rental property a few years ago!

CHAPTER 4:

Options Trading

What are Options

An option is a contract that gives the buyer the right to buy or sell an underlying asset at a specified price on or before a specified date. It is a binding contract with very strictly defined terms. Here's a very easy example: Let's say you find a super sexy Chevy Corvette z06 that you just have to buy. Unfortunately, you don't have the cash right now, but you will in two months. You talk to the owner and agree on a deal that gives you the option to buy that car in two months for a price of $50,000. Since you don't have the cash up front, the owner makes you pay $2,000 for this option.

A few different scenarios can take place in those two months:

Scenario 1: Let's say it's discovered that the car actually has a factory upgrade that it wasn't supposed to have. Now it's the only z06 in the world with this upgrade, so it's a one of a kind car and is now worth $200,000! Since the owner sold you the option, he is contractually bound to sell you the car for the agreed upon $50,000. You just made a profit of $148,000 ($200,000 current value - $50,000 purchase price - $2,000 option = $148,000). Not bad.

—Juch

Scenario 2: It's discovered that car is actually a lemon with a salvage title. It's only worth $5,000. Although you originally fell in love with the car, it's not all you once thought it was. Even though you bought the option, you as the buyer are under no obligation to go through with the sale. You only forfeit the $2,000 price of the option.

These scenarios exemplify the two most important aspects of options. When you buy an option, you have the right to buy the asset, but not the obligation. You can simply let the expiration date pass, at which point the option has no value. It also demonstrates that an option is merely a contract that deals in an underlying asset (in this case, the Corvette). This is why options are often referred to as derivatives — they derive their value from something else.

Types of Options

When it comes to stocks, there are two types of options available: calls and puts.

Call Option: A call option gives you the right to buy shares. You make money as a stock rises in price. You are hoping the stock will increase in price substantially before the option expires.

Put Option: A put option gives you the right to sell shares. You make money as a stock drops in price. You are hoping that the price of the stock falls before your option expires.

That's the great thing about options — they allow you to make money as something goes up in value, or even as something goes down in value.

Let's take a look at an example. Let's say we have a company called Tucker's Agency. On June 1, the stock price of Tucker's Agency is $50 and the premium (cost of the option contract) is $2 with an expiration date of August 15th and a strike price of $55. Because each option contract represents 100 shares, the total price of your contract would be $2 X 100 = $200.

The strike price is the price a stock must go above (for calls) or below (for puts) before a position can be exercised for a profit. In this the contract, the strike price is $55, so the stock must rise above $55 before a call option is worth anything. And since your contract is $2 per share, the actual break-even price $57.

Four weeks later, the stock price is at $60. The options contract has increased and is now worth $6. $6 X 100 = $600. Subtract what you initially paid for the contract and your profit is $400 (($6 - $2) X 100 = $400). You have just doubled your money, but only if you decided to actually sell when the price of the stock was $60. If you decided not to exercise your option and the stock then dropped to $45 by the expiration date, you would lose your initial investment of $200.

How to Analyze Trades

Sean Allison, the creator of www.incomegeneratorstrategy.com, has come up with a formula for buying and selling options that is truly remarkable. He has used this formula to generate $25,000 per month for himself while only working 15 hours per week, in addition to the money he makes teaching his system to his students. Not only that, he has a success rate of 70% on his trades!

When I spoke to him, he mentioned that what most people don't understand is the flow of money. It took him several years to get this idea firmly implanted in his brain, but essentially, it's understanding correlations among different financial sectors and learning where the flow of money is. Because money is always flowing from one sector to another, one asset class to another, the key is understanding the direction of the money flow and then setting up your options strategy accordingly.

There is an indicator in market analysis called OBV, or On-Balance Volume, that can be very useful when analyzing the flow of money. OBV is a momentum indicator that uses volume flow to predict changes in stock price. When OBV is moving up, it indicates that buying pressure is exceeding selling pressure. This indicator was developed in the 1960s by a man named Joseph Granville, who believed that when volume increases sharply without a significant change in the price of the stock, the price will eventually jump upward, and vice versa.

Let's take government bonds for example, which are a very safe place to put your money. When bonds go down in value, the return you can get from a bond actually goes up. If the bonds go down, the return for the bonds, or the yields, goes up. As a result, people sell those shares, and the money flows into bonds. Just understanding things like that relationship can allow you as a savvy investor to make an awful lot of money.

Sean recently taught this correlation to some of his elite students, and one particular student took it to heart. Using Sean's advice, the student made over $3,500 dollars in bonds with one trade. This kind of success rests on understanding the correlations of where the flow of money is coming from, and then utilizing options as your investment vehicle.

One thing that Sean learned during his time as a fundamental analysis investor was that you can't trust what you see on the stock charts. His job was looking at a company and determining whether it was a good, profitable company that was likely to grow its earnings over time. What he realized, though, is that that information can be manipulated. Companies like Enron were showing very good fundamentals up until the day they collapsed.

Sean's strategy has some basic steps to follow. The first thing to look at is the charts. You have to understand in which direction the overall market is going. Is the overall market moving higher, or is it moving lower? The charts and the technical analysis will enable you to determine that.

Once that's done, then you can narrow your focus to a particular sector. Find out what the best performing sector is — or what the worst performing sector is, depending on whether you want to make money on something gaining value or something losing value.

First the overall market; then the sector; and finally, zero in on stocks that are the weakest or strongest in their particular sector. If you want to make money as stocks fall in price, track down the lowest stocks. If you want to make money as a stock rises in price, determine the stocks that are the strongest in their sector.

From that analysis, you'll be able to determine an entry point and, more importantly, an exit point if the trade doesn't work out. This step is all about risk management, and it is imperative. If you can become an effective risk manager, you'll make a lot of money in this business. The key, according to Sean, is to limit the downside and maximize the upside.

For Sean, there's the most money to be made when a stock is going down in price – which is a very difficult concept for the average person to understand. Many people have an automatic panic response when they hear that a stock is falling in price, so it's difficult for them to understand just how much money there is to be made with this method. When a stock comes down in price, it tends to move down quickly, and that's exactly what enables Sean and his students to make money very quickly as a result.

Sean's primary means of finding opportunities to make money is the charts. Technical analysis is hugely important to achieve success with this strategy, because charting is, more than anything, a reflection of human emotion. Many times, a stock's price will move in a way that, frankly, defies logic. The company is producing the same amount of goods, has the same amount of employees – but the price can change dramatically, based more than anything else on human emotion and how people feel about the company. If you understand how to read charts, you'll be able to see the flow of money across the market and the element of human emotion in play.

How to Implement Those Trades

Once you've determined the overall market trend and focused in on a particular sector, you're ready to pick out a stock. From there, Sean advises setting up an income trade.

This will enable you to have the profit objectives as well as your risk management set up early on, so that everything is in place at the same time that you place the trade.

At this stage, something that Sean calls trading psychology comes into play. It is the single most important factor of implementing this strategy successfully. He explained in our interview that there's something about this type of trade that goes against the grain of human psychology. After all, as intelligent individuals, we understand that any trade we make could go wrong at any time. The most logical response to this uncertainty is, "Then why would you do it?" But, as Sean points out, that's part of the game: understanding that this is a game of probability, and that, as investors, we're simply playing the probabilities.

To play the probabilities effectively, your own emotion has to be taken out of the equation as much as possible. Check your ego at the door, too — you're not trying to force your opinion on the stocks or trying to make the markets give you money. What you are doing is using mathematics and a sound understanding of trading psychology to consistently make money while mitigating risk. Knowing that you could be wrong at any time, and then risk-managing against that, is the make-or-break skill of this kind of venture.

How do you defeat the problems caused by emotion-clouded judgment? Sean believes he's found the true enemy, and the enemy is us. We're greedy, we're fearful, we're indecisive – all the same things that rule the stock market. To be able to counteract all those illogical influences, you must have a clear, levelheaded focus on your goals and what you expect to get out of each and every trade.

Say, for example, that you're looking to retire. That means you're not looking to get rich quick — you're looking for a stable investment that can provide you with financial support. Keying into your goals for a trade lets you set a specific profit target and a specific price for the stock to move to. Remember, you can't set out just hoping that a trade will turn out "good" without thinking about what that really means for you in your particular situation. To get the results you need, you need to know exactly what your parameters are. It's important is to set a reasonable profit target, and as soon as it hits that level, have the trade closed out automatically. This system takes the biggest enemy out of trading: us.

Just as important is setting downside parameters, so that you know when it's time to cut your losses before you lose any more money. You need to acknowledge that anything can happen in the market. If you do, then you're always going to set a target to take your profits, as well as define the exact moment that you'll pull out on a trade. Doing so is what allows you to keep your losses small and keep your profits growing. That's the real key to risk management.

Let's take a look at a specific example that Sean shared. First, he looks at a specific market or index, and then tries to find strong stock candidates within that index.

In this example, he was interested in Google, so he focused in on the NASDAQ. Take a look at the notes in his chart. A few positive factors were identified: first, the NASDAQ broke above resistance with the news that the Federal Reserve would be keeping interest rates steady. Second, the OBV, or On-Balance Volume, is trending upward, which indicates that buying pressure is exceeding selling pressure.

60

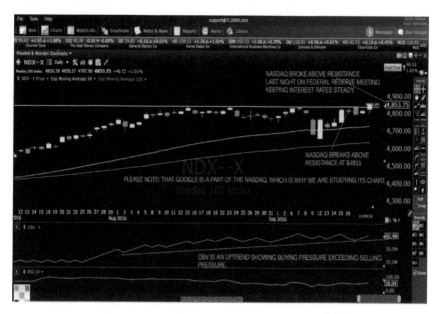

Then Sean moves to the individual stock charts. Google and Amazon had been performing strongly, and since the NASDAQ was performing strongly as well, he decided to place the trade. In the analysis charts below, EMA is the Exponential Moving Average. EMA is a stock chart tool investors use to watch trends in the price of a stock.

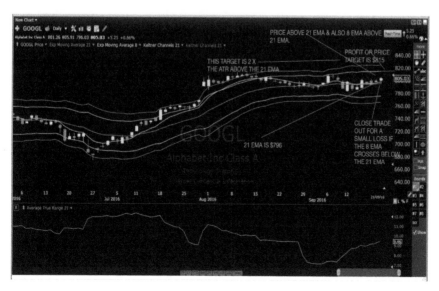

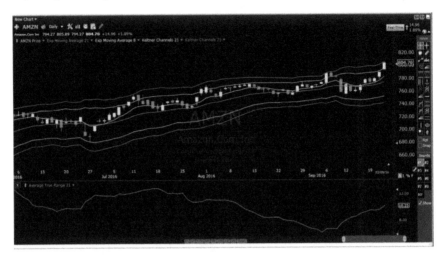

Sean recommended both Google and Amazon to his students based on his analysis of the above charts. He sets up the profit target and maximum loss all at the same time. Again, this is the key to keeping a professional and consistent approach. It keeps human emotion out of the trade and automates the process as much as possible.

What were the results? You won't believe this. Sean se
example from one of his students who took his advice an
these very same trades.

Trade Date	Action	Symbol/Desc.	Qty	Price	Comm.	Net Amount	Gain/Loss for symbol
AMAZON							
09/22/2016	STC	AMZN SepWk4 790 Call	5	$9.75	$14.95	$4,859.83	
09/21/2016	BTO	AMZN SepWk4 790 Call	5	$3.22	$14.95	($1,625.07)	3,234.76
Net Realized Gain/Loss for AMZN							$3,234.76
ALPHABET							
09/22/2016	STC	GOOGL SepWk4 805 Call	5	$6.87	$14.95	$3,419.86	
09/21/2016	BTO	GOOGL SepWk4 805 Call	5	$3.10	$14.95	($1,565.06)	1,854.80
Net Realized Gain/Loss for GOOGL							$1,854.80
TOTAL REALIZED GAIN/LOSS							$5,089.56

Analysis Data For 9/22/2016 - 9/23/2016　　　　View Annual Analysis Summary

That's right. One of his students made $5,089.56 from this exact
trade.

Key Takeaways

The biggest thing Sean said he has learned in his life is that you have
to find a mentor. By his own calculation, he probably invested around
$250,000 on programs that didn't work to find a way to make money
outside of his job. The problem with this method is the same one
that so many other people who attend these lectures and seminars
discover too late — you spend money on a program and assume that
the "expert" knows what they're talking about, when in reality, they
don't actually make any money off of the strategies they're teaching
you. Sean's advice is to find a mentor who actually makes a living
doing exactly what they teach.

*"Without a mentor your VERY BEST thinking has got you exactly where you
are today."* – Raymond Aaron

If the teaching is all theory-based, it's simply not useful. Talk is cheap.
Sean mentioned a student of his that had five degrees, including a

PhD. This lady was an academic, and she loved to study and analyze things. The problem was that she would analyze things to the point of taking no action. She had been a very good student and she'd really studied. After about a year, Sean asked, "How's your trading?" She said, "I haven't actually placed any trades yet."

Her goal had been to fully understand everything there was to know about stock market trading before she took any action. Sean thinks that's the wrong way to do it. With Sean's help, the student placed two trades, and in her first month she made $10,000. In her own words, she learned more in that one month than an entire year of studying theory.

Sean emphasized that the best way for you to learn options trading is to actually do it. He's a huge proponent of starting with small trades as early as you can. The sooner you start trading with live money, the sooner you'll start to see results.

CHAPTER 5:

eBooks

Creating an eBook is typically the first step that eager entrepreneurs take when starting out online. Why? It's fast, it's cheap, and it takes minimal skill to write an eBook.

"Why not go through the front door of success? To do that, publish a book. Nothing will raise your status like a book. It's instant credibility. It will help you leave your legacy, inspire your audience, and motivate the world. It will get people fired up, it will communicate your mission and start a movement." – Craig Ballantyne

As soon as you begin to sell products, you put a dent in the cycle of exchanging your time for money. In the introduction, I mentioned that 99% of people exchange their time for money, which means they always have to go back to work if they want to get paid. Think about it — you write an eBook once, and it can continually make you money with no further effort involved.

Every new eBook you put together becomes a new stream of income for you. This reminds me of something I've read over and over again: "The typical millionaire has around 7 streams of income." Create an eBook and you are well on your way to that magic number! Create a second book, and there's a second stream of income. It's that simple.

The profit margins on eBooks can be 100%. As they are a digital product, you eliminate inventory, overhead, shipping, and the other prohibitive entry costs of physical books. It doesn't matter if you sell one or 25,000 — the costs to you won't change.

Since it's all online, you also have the entire world as your marketplace. Your pool of potential customers is no longer constricted to your state, country, or even your continent. You instantly gain access to the entire global market of consumers.

Mark Anastasi, author of the New York Times bestseller "The Laptop Millionaire," used precisely this strategy to go from homeless to making $330 per day in just a few weeks. I was lucky enough to interview him, and he shared his formula for successfully creating eBooks.

How to Get Started

It seems like everyone who has written a book about eBooks, or even eBooks on eBooks, has their own "best" strategy, but they all boil down to the same basic steps.

1. Find a Target Market

2. Find Out What That Market Wants or Needs

3. Give it to Them

Sounds easy enough. Let's talk about each step in more detail below.

Find a Market

What is a market? A market is a group of individuals that are all interested in the same thing. Let's say one of your hobbies is collecting rocks. I know you thought you were alone with your strange obsession, but believe it or not, there are plenty of other individuals out there who love collecting rocks just as much as you do! That's a market.

Have you had a termite, ant, or rodent infestation in your house that you were able to solve without having to call an exterminator by using a clever home remedy? There are thousands of people with infestations that they would LOVE to get rid of. If you found a way for them to do it, there's your market. Better yet, because you were able to solve that problem without an exterminator, your product can not only get rid of people's infestations, it can also save them money! That is how you deliver serious value.

The best way to find a market is to choose something that you yourself are interested in. That way, you'll never get tired of creating products and you will actually want to serve that market. To find potential markets, think about:

- What are you interested in?

- What do you do with your friends?

- What subject do you consider yourself an expert at?

- What is your favorite sport?

- What problems of your own have you solved?

The list goes on and on. Anything that is being searched for online is a market. The smaller the market, the more "niche" it is. There are broad markets, and there are niches, and there are niches of niches — the possibilities are endless. One of the best ways to figure out what is being searched for online is to go to Google Adwords (https://www.google.com/adwords/).

All you have to do to get started is create an account. Once you are signed in, you'll be taken to the first step, "About Your Business." It doesn't really matter what you put here — just move on to step 2, "Your First Campaign." This is where you input your keywords. See below.

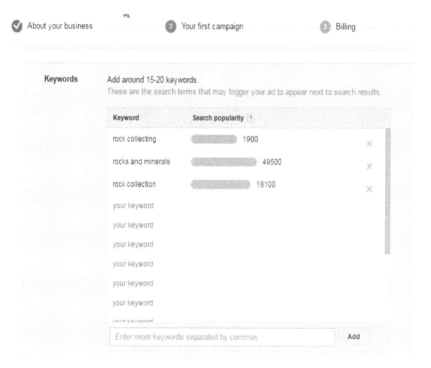

Turns out collecting rocks isn't such a strange obsession after all! With a total of 69,500 monthly searches for just those three keywords, it's actually a pretty strong market. Do you see how valuable this tool can be? At this point, there is no need to go any further with the tool, unless you want to do searches for fun (which, I have to admit, I have done. It's quite enlightening to see how many people are searching for the same things you are).

You want to find a market of rabid hobbyists — people that are so passionate about their niche that they will buy anything and everything related to it. A great source to find these rabid hobbyists is www.meetup.com. This website lists groups all over the world. The website claims to have 27.47 million members who make up of 255,791 groups across 179 countries. It's a fantastic resource to find hobbyists for every passion under the sun. Not only can you join the groups that interest you, you can also find people to interview about the next topic you're researching.

Once you have identified a possible market, there are a few questions you will want to ask yourself before moving forward.

Question 1 – Is the market large enough for your product?

You want to stay somewhere between 30,000 to 100,000 searches on Google per month. Even a strong 10,000 or 6,000 search market can make you money because a smaller niche means fewer sales, but it also means you can charge a higher price. The more specialized you get, the more those people are willing to pay for your product. Believe it or not, you can actually tap into a "micro-niche" and make a fortune, but your market still has to reach a certain size for this to work.

Question 2 – Does this market have money?

This may seem obvious, but you would be surprised at how often people don't think about this question before they starting writing their book. If you write an eBook about how to help poor, impoverished teens in foster homes find great parents, your market is poor, impoverished teens. No matter how helpful your information is, that market has no money to spend on your product. You must make sure your target market has disposable income.

Question 3 – Is there good back-end potential?

Back-end potential means that once the customers have made the initial purchase, are there more products and services you can sell them down the road, ideally at higher price points? According to www.invespcro.com, it costs five times as much to attract a new customer as it does to keep an existing one.[2] Not only that, but the site also goes on to say that the probability of selling to an existing customer is 60-70%, while the probability of selling to a new prospect is 5-20%. Existing customers are also 50% more likely to try new products and spend 31% more when compared to new customers. Basically, once you make a few sales, YOUR EXISTING CUSTOMERS ARE YOUR BUSINESS.

It is imperative that you find a market that wants to buy your product, and that you find a problem within that market that you can solve. One of the big mistakes people make is that they come up with a topic they enjoy or that they know a lot about. Then they spend weeks or months creating the product, and *then* they look at who would want to buy it. It has to be done the other way around. Find your buyers first. Create your product second.

Find Out What That Market Wants

How do you find out what your market wants? Research, research, research. This is extremely important. You don't want to spend weeks putting together a book about "How to Install Widget Software XYZ on Windows 10," only to find another video about the EXACT same thing. I'm not saying that you necessarily need to find an untapped market, but if there is an exact replica product out there, you want to know about it sooner rather than later.

One of the main reasons people go online is to find an answer to their problem. So you can go to Google and type in things like:

- How to

- Tutorial

- Step by Step

2

http://www.invespcro.com/blog/customer-acquisition-retention/

- Instructions

- Tips

Of course, you need to make these searches specific to your niche. "How to collect rocks," "the step by step guide to rocks," etc. If your niche is consistently searching for instructions on starting an ant farm, you should provide those instructions. If someone else has already done so, do it better with more detail, or add videos. Find a way to make your product stand out.

You can even research what products related to your niche sell the best. Investigate the following questions:

- What products sell the best on eBay?

- What products sell the best on Amazon?

- What books sell the best on Kindle?

How can those questions help you? Let's say that you go to Amazon and a book called "How to Fix a Light Bulb" is a best seller — but the book is 10 years old now. Update it! That market obviously has demand, and they need something current, so this is a perfect opportunity.

You can even set up a squeeze, or flycatcher, page. A flycatcher page is a website where you ask your potential customers, or even current customers, what topics should be covered in your next eBook, or what questions they may have about your niche. They will type in their answers, and you get their feedback straight to your inbox. Now you know what your market wants!

Give it To Them

Now this is where you create your content and do your marketing.

Step 1: Capture Your Content

This can be done in a multitude of ways:

Squeeze Page

As I mentioned previously, a squeeze (or flycatcher) page can be a great tool. Once you get the answers back from your market, filter them down to the 10 most common questions that people have about your niche. Make each question its own chapter. Then answer their questions. There's your 10-chapter eBook!

Start Writing

If you are already an expert on the topic you're writing about, come up with a few things you want to discuss and start writing! The key is to come up with an outline of your topics. If you don't like writing, turn on a recorder and just start talking about your subject. The key is to get your content out into the open. Do NOT worry about grammatical errors or typos at this point. Again, you just want to get everything out there.

Interview Experts

If you don't know enough about your topic, you can always interview people who do. This is one of the best product creation strategies out there. All you need to do is research who the experts are in your niche. Just go to Google and type in "niche" and "expert." Once you find some experts in your niche, politely ask them for an interview. Most of them will be flattered and say yes, especially if your niche is a tiny one that doesn't get a lot of publicity.

Once you find an expert who is willing to do an interview, come up with a list of questions to ask them, get your recording software ready, and call them for the interview. That first interview can easily become your first chapter. Find nine more experts and now you have another 10-chapter eBook filled with expert advice! All you have to do is transcribe the recordings (which you can outsource to someone on www.upwork.com — you can even use Upwork to find someone to write the entire 10-chapter eBook for you based on the interviews) and convert it into a nice, neat chapter format. The best part about this process is even if you knew nothing about growing lima beans, now that you've interviewed 10 experts on growing lima beans and written an eBook about it, you are considered an expert on growing lima beans!

Not only that, but now you have recordings of experts in your niche that you can upload to your website. You can charge a membership fee to your site in order to get the full interviews with the experts. This is how you start to upsell your existing customers.

Buy Private Label Rights (PLR) eBooks

Private label rights eBooks are products that have already been written and are now being sold. When you buy PLR products, you are buying the rights to change anything you want in the product, sell it, and keep all the money.

For example, you could find a PLR product on growing lima beans with a boring title. Switch up the title to something catchy, put your name and picture on it, create a website for it, and start selling.

You can even buy three or four PLR products, combine them into one product, and there's another eBook ready to go!

License Products

Licensing products doesn't involve any product creation on your end. Instead, you are licensing someone else's product. Let's say you read an eBook and absolutely love it. You just reach out to creator of that product and offer a certain amount to license it. If they agree, that means that you now have the right to sell the product and keep 100% of the profits!

Expert Suggestions

Mark also provided some tips on creating an eBook that sells extremely well:

1. Don't get hung up about how good your writing is, or how much credibility you have in your niche. It really comes down to how much value your book has to your customers.

74

2. Create a great headline. Mark terms this a "Million Dollar Marketing Hook." The title of the book is extremely important. For instance, you could call your eBook "Twitter Marketing" or "Twitter Secrets Revealed." Those are decent titles, but what's even better is something with amounts and deadlines. For example: "How to Get 100,000 Twitter Followers in 30 days." That's a title that will sell. 90% of the success of a book comes down to the headline.

3. Choose a topic that people are irrationally and passionately interested in. You want to tap into consumers who are excited to find a solution, right now. There are three major information markets that fit the bill — products that have to do with making money or business success, products about health or weight loss, and any product that has to do with relationships and love.

Step 2: Edit Your Content

Now that you have captured all of your raw information, you need to transform the data into a presentable product.

Make sure you are keeping the knowledge and skill level of your target demographic in mind. If you're writing a how-to guide for beginners, make sure you are very detailed about every step along the way. Avoid jargon specific to your niche, or make sure to define it the first time it's used.

Make sure that your content flows logically. That's why an outline is so important. With an outline, you can lay out all the chapters of your book in order, and then start writing. It's not impossible to do it the other way around, but you will probably waste time going back and reshuffling things later on.

Once you have everything together, the next step is to show your document to someone else with fresh eyes and get their honest evaluation. It's best to avoid spouses or parents for this part, because there's a good chance they'll tell you it's great regardless of how awful it is. You want an unbiased opinion.

Step 3: Deliver Your Content

This is the big piece of the puzzle that's missing for most beginners, and the reason they don't even bother trying to create a product in the first place. Should you create a website first? Do you list the eBook online first? What is the process supposed to look like? Let's put the steps in order for you.

Create your website

The first step in creating your website is to choose a good domain name. A domain name is your web address. For example, www.thepassiveincomemachine.com is my domain name. Choosing your domain is extremely important. You must pick a domain name that accurately reflects your niche and makes sense to your market. Don't choose pizza.com if your product is about burgers.

Don't worry about getting too specific in your web address. Think about the people that are searching the internet: if they are just browsing, they will search for very broad terms like "noodles" or "trucks." But if they actually want to BUY a product, they will search for the particular product they have in mind, like "2016 Ford F-150 FX4 under 100,000 miles for sale." The smaller your niche, and the more tailored your web address, the better chance you have of being at the top of the Google search results for someone who is looking to make a purchase.

Another important factor in your domain name is to always choose ".com" names (as opposed to .biz, .net, .guru, etc. — there are actually a lot of options out there). Most people assume that .com is the ending to your website name, so that's what they type in the address bar. If your site is actually ".org" and not ".com," the customers will end up at someone else's site, and you definitely don't want that. It's just like if you've ever thought you remembered a 1-800 number, but when you get home and dial, you get something completely different because the number you actually want is a 1-888 number. See the problem? Stick with ".com."

Once you have your domain name, you need to set up your website hosting. You don't need to pay someone lots of money for this; there are fantastic hosting services out there for less than $5/month. Check out www.godaddy.com or www.bluehost.com as some starting points.

The best part about both of the hosting providers I just mentioned is that they also provide website builders, typically for free, when you purchase a domain name or hosting services. They have pre-made template websites to choose from and modify for your own website. No need to get hung up on this step — just pick one and go!

By the way, you can also pay someone on www.fiverr.com to create your website for you, typically for less than $100. You just tell them everything you want the website to say or do, and they create it for you.

Create a Sales Page

A sales page is a landing page on your website that details why the customer needs to purchase your product. This is what most information marketers use to sell their products. Why? Because it works.

There is a pretty specific formula for sale pages that has been used for decades. From infomercials on TV to websites, this formula is almost always the exact same, and that's because the formula works. If it ain't broke, don't fix it.

1. Present the Problem: What problem is your target market having?

2. Lead Up to Your Solution: What if there was a way to solve this problem?

3. Present Your eBook: Reveal your eBook and tell your audience it's exactly what they've been looking for to solve that problem.

4. Insert Testimonials: When people think they are missing out, it makes them want to join.

5. List the Benefits of Your eBook, Not the Features: List the desired outcomes your market has. "Lose weight." "Save money."

6. Make Your Offer: Tell them exactly what they are going to get for the price. "Discounted 65% off of retail value!"

7. List Your Bonuses: Always include something extra. Still have those interview recordings somewhere?

8. Include a Guarantee: Always include a guarantee. "30-Day Money Back Guarantee."

9. Add Scarcity: "Limited Time Offer" or "Call in the next 90 minutes before we run out!"

10. Tell Them Exactly What To Do: Some people do what they're told. It's that simple. "Don't forget to add the product to your cart and make the purchase! No better time than right now!"

If you can't create a great sales letter yourself, consider hiring a professional to do it for you. This is arguably the most important part of the process, so spending a few bucks for a talented sales writer can reap huge dividends down the line.

How Do You Price Your Product?

The general rules of thumb when pricing your product are to:

1. Develop a high-quality product rather than a low-priced one.

2. Avoid products under $30.

3. Aim to break even with only 15-20 sales.

4. Price your products based on the value it provides for the client, not on how much it costs to produce.

Remember, people generally associate price with quality. You aren't trying to beat Wal-Mart's price — you are pricing based on the amount of value you have delivered.

When you go into a store and see two of the same products on the shelves, but one is 50% off, you immediately ask an employee, "What's wrong with this one?" Don't set the price too low on your product; remember, it's full of VALUE.

How Do You Sell Your Product?

You can't get your eBook into customers' hands if they can't find it.

List it everywhere! You can turn a single eBook into 100 different income streams. You can list it on your own website, on Amazon, eBay, Clickbank, Apple iStore, Lulu, Nook Press, Smashwords, Lightning Source, BookBaby — the list is endless.

For even more places to list, buy some recording software and record yourself reading your book. Then, sell it on iTunes, Audible.com, Amazon, or Audiobooks.com.

Once you get the eBook online, you can use some Pay-Per-Click advertising with Google Adwords to drive traffic to your website. Just like we used Google Adwords earlier to figure out our niche, we can finish the process with those same keywords for marketing. Remember to stay very specific with your keywords. It does no good to pay for advertising when people who want to buy race cars are finding your website about donkeys.

Facebook ads can be a fantastic opportunity because Facebook is able to target an extremely specific type of person to display your ad to. You can set your target to something like "single women between the ages of 25-35 who enjoy hiking and live in Texas." With that level of detail, you can have highly focused ads through Facebook.

You can reach out to blogs you enjoy, or research blogs in your niche and contact the owners. You typically have to pay them upfront, but this is another great way to get good, targeted advertising.

One of the best ways to get more customers is by setting up an affiliate program. An affiliate is someone who advertises your book for you, and you pay them a commission every time they make a sale. Using affiliates is typically much more effective than any other advertising source. You have a stranger who is extremely motivated (because they get paid) trying to sell your book for you. It's fantastic!

www.clickbank.com is probably the most popular affiliate marketplace in the world. How does it work? You just sign up to sell your eBook on Clickbank, and they already have an affiliate program built in. You send out your offer and affiliates respond to you. You can choose to pay them 20% - 75% commission. If you offer a low commission, they won't be as incentivized as they will be with a 75% commission. The more you're offering them, the more they'll want to sell your product.

Mark provided an example of a woman he knew who was generating around $1,000,000 per year from eBooks alone. He mentioned that when he first started, he was only selling on ClickBank, nothing else. Then he attended a seminar where this woman was speaking.

She had about 120 books on Amazon and other platforms, and she was making about a million dollars a year from these 120 books. She would pay writers to create a book, with a cost to her of about $700 per finished eBook.

The message of her talk was this — why only sell on ClickBank? You can sell on ClickBank for a start, but you can also sell the same book on Amazon Kindle, through Lightning Source as a physical book, through Smashwords with the Apple network, on iTunes, and more. Why not sell it through the eBook platforms like Kobo, Lulu, Draft 2 Digital, Ingram, Noble, PubIt, Book Tango, Book Baby, and Nook Press?

Mark has now compiled a list of 100 different booksellers and book publishing platforms. Through these platforms, Mark and his company sell both eBooks and physical books to a massive audience of readers.

He went on to explain that they are also selling these books through ACX. The website acx.com allows eBook sellers to upload the audiobook version of their book and sell it through Amazon, Audible, and iTunes. Besides this, Mark also encouraged entrepreneurs to think about creating a video course of their book if it's a how-to or informational guide. Video courses can be sold through Udemy, Lola, or other similar sites.

If you can successfully tap into several of these platforms, instead of just having one income stream from your eBook through Clickbank, now you can sell it across 100 different online booksellers and book publishing platforms. eBook publishing platforms, audiobook selling platforms, video course selling platforms – these are just some of the income streams you can derive from your book.

Mark said he even knows people who make good money from selling their video courses at a discount through Groupon and numerous other "Deal of the Day" sites. With this multi-platform approach, you can take a single eBook and turn it into 120 different streams of income.

How Do You Drive Traffic To Your eBook?

Google Adwords is the most common way to drive traffic to your site. In my interview with Mark, he said he was paying about $0.05 per click, which means for every $5 he was spending on Adwords, he would get 100 visitors to his site. Two out of those 100 were buying his product. That means for every $5 of advertising, he was generating $134 in revenue (his first eBook on natural treatment for diabetes was $67). He went from making zero to five sales per week with Google Adwords.

For this first book, Mark also used Clickbank and found affiliates to help him sell. He agreed to split the proceeds from each sale 50/50 with the affiliates. They did the advertising for the book by creating blogs and websites to drive traffic, and they did it all for free in exchange for their commissions. This is why it's extremely important to give affiliates at least 50% commission. If you don't, they won't have any reason to work hard to sell your book. For the most productive relationship with your affiliates, they need to have some skin in the game.

So how can you generate $100K per year with eBooks?

You've identified a great market, you've interviewed the experts, and you've got your book out online to sell. Great! If it sells enough to make you $100K, congrats! But the easiest, most foolproof way to make six figures with eBooks is the backend potential.

Let's say you sell 100 copies of your eBook. Now, do you have other things that you can offer those 100 clients on your mailing list? Can you offer them coaching? Can you sell them a seminar? Can you sell them another course? Can you sell them a different course every month? Can you get them interested in a membership site?

The idea is to find something that will allow you to continue your relationship with that buyer, something that will allow you to help them further or faster in regard to a problem you addressed in your first eBook.

The majority of the profit in any business is typically on the backend. You make the frontend sale for $20, $30, $40, $50, or $60 — but the largest portion of your profit is going to be in what you can sell after that, in increments of $200, $300, and $500.

Remember what I said a few pages earlier about your existing customers? According to www.invespcro.com, it costs five times as much to attract a new customer than to keep an existing one.[3] While the probability of selling to a new prospect is 5-20%, the probability of selling to an existing customer is 60-70%. Existing customers are also 50% more likely to try new products, and they typically spend 31% more money compared to a new customer. Basically, once you make a few sales, YOUR EXISTING CUSTOMERS ARE YOUR BUSINESS.

100 *existing* customers can be worth far more than 20,000 *potential* customers

Here's a real life example of this in action. Mark provided some numbers for his book, "The Laptop Millionaire." That book was published in 2012. It sold over 100,000 copies and topped $1.7 million in 12 weeks. The key to this success was the upsell with his seminar. Readers loved the book and wanted to know more, so the upsell seminars that Mark offered were a huge success.

In another example, he interviewed 12 Facebook marketers to find out how to make money on Facebook. He published his findings as an eBook and launched it on ClickBank. That one eBook generated $400,000 in 30 days. The revenue was comprised of 5,000 buyers in those 30 days, with an upsell in addition to the book. Accessing backend potential with well-placed upsells is the key to making serious money with eBooks.

3

http://www.invespcro.com/blog/customer-acquisition-retention/

CHAPTER 6:
Membership Sites

Membership sites are a fantastic way to earn money online. The most obvious benefit of owning a membership site is, of course, the recurring monthly payments rolling in to you. In addition, if you can get a decent membership base, it's not uncommon for membership sites to sell for six figures.

Membership Site Benefits

There are numerous benefits to creating a membership site, but here are some of the main ones:

Increased Revenue: The financial payouts of membership sites can be substantial. It's basically like selling one product, then getting paid over and over for that product every month. All you need is a small base of members to make some serious cash. If you only have 200 members, but they are paying you $25 per month, you're bringing in $5,000!

Customer Loyalty: When you're selling a product, you don't really get a chance to build a solid relationship with that customer. But if they become a member, you can deliver more value to them on a weekly or monthly basis and build loyalty. It is much easier to sell new products or services to an existing customer who trusts you than to sell to a prospect.

No Tangible Products: The main product with just about all membership sites is information. The best part about delivering your member's information, instead of an actual product, is that information is free. It takes no overhead except the cost of running the site

How To Create A Membership Site for Free

I am going to create a brand new membership site from scratch to show you the process. I am using BlueHost for my domain and hosting services in this example. These instructions assume you already have a website, or that you know how to set up a site using WordPress. If not, head on over to BlueHost, GoDaddy, or HostGator to get your domain and hosting set up. Be sure that your site is based on the WordPress platform, because we are going to be using a WordPress membership plugin that will take care of most of the backend details that are required for running a membership site.

Free Membership Site Software

Once you get your site and hosting set up with WordPress, log in as Admin to your site. In your WordPress dashboard, go to Plugins > Add new. In the search box, type in "S2member" and hit search.

Select the S2Member Framework plugin and install it on your site.

From everything I have read, S2Member seems to be the best membership site software out there. The company offers a completely free version as well as a paid version. The free version is more than adequate for the majority of site owners, as it offers functionalities including integration with some of the top payment gateways such as PayPal, Clickbank, Authorize.net, and others.

Once you get it installed, you will see it listed on your installed plugins page.

Before you adjust the settings to get it set up correctly, let's talk about how S2Member works.

1. When a visitor decides they want to join, they will be routed to a Membership Options page. This is where the details such as price or service will be located, as well as the actual payment buttons for them to subscribe.

2. When that visitor clicks the PayPal button it will route them to the PayPal site, where the visitor agrees to the payment and double checks that the details are accurate. Once the payment is finalized, they are returned to your site where you provide them a username and password, or they can choose themselves. From there, they can log in to the member's area. They will also get an automatically generated email that has additional instructions.

3. The first page they will land on is the Login Welcome page. This is where you can direct them to other areas of the site. If a visitor who isn't a member yet tries to access any of the protected pages, they will automatically be directed to the membership options page, which is a great feature.

4. The plugin handles all of this automatically for you. From billing, to subscriptions, to cancellations — it's all taken care of.

Setting Up the Site

The first step in this process is to create two pages.

On the Pages tab of your site, click "Add New."

1. A "Subscribe" page – this is the membership options page. Once you type in the name of the page, select Publish.

2. A "Members" page – this is the page new members will be routed to after signing up.

Once you've added these pages, we can set up the rest of the site. Here are the steps:

- In the dashboard, click on the S2Member tab.

- Find "General Options" and click on it.

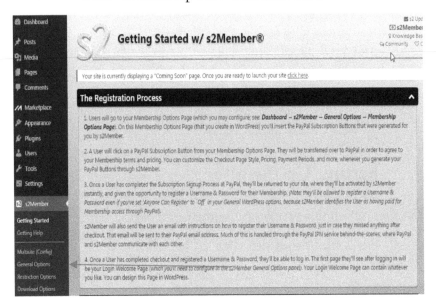

Once you click the "General Options" button, you will be presented with every option you have for configuring the settings to your liking.

Let's go tab by tab and configure the settings…

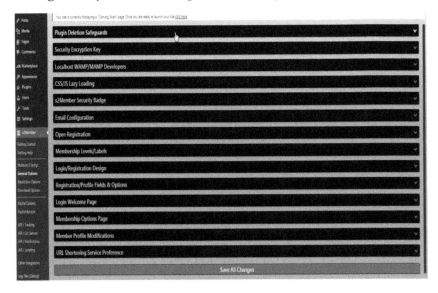

1. **Plugin Deletion Safeguards**: This should be preset to Yes for you. If not, select Yes.

2. **Security Encryption Key**: Click on "Auto Generate." This will automatically generate an encryption key for you. The key will be a crazy long series of letters, numbers, and special values. I strongly suggest that you copy and paste this somewhere safe.

3. **Localhost WAMP/MAMP Developers**: Unless you are setting up S2Member in a local host, this won't affect you. You can simply ignore this option.

4. **CSS/JS Lazy Loading**: This will be defaulted to No. Leave as is.

5. **S2Member Security Badge**: This depends on whether or not you want to display a security badge on your site. Totally optional. For the sake of this exercise, we will leave it as the default No.

6. **Email Configuration:** The emails should default to the information you provided upon setup. The Email From: "Name" will be preset as your site title – this is the name/address that will appear in outgoing email notifications sent by the S2Member plugin. If you want to use a different email than the one you registered with, enter it in the "Email From Address" field. The "New User Email Configuration" can be left at No, which is the default.

7. **Open Registration:** If you are offering a free membership option, then you will select Yes. If not, and you are only offering paid membership options, then enter No.

8. **Membership Levels/Labels:** This is where you would define what you want to call your different membership levels (i.e. Bronze, Silver, Gold, etc.). You can leave them at the default labels for now.

9. **Login/Registration Design:** The S2Member plugin uses the standard WordPress login forms, but you can customize the login page to whatever you want. You can change the background color, the size, the font, and even add logos.

10. **Registration/Profile Fields & Options:** This allows you to decide if the members can customize their own passwords and display names. It's best to let their display name be a username of their choice, as some members may not want their full names displayed. If you want to let members set their own passwords, switch the third option (Allow Custom Passwords during Registration?) to Yes. You can leave the other options to their defaults.

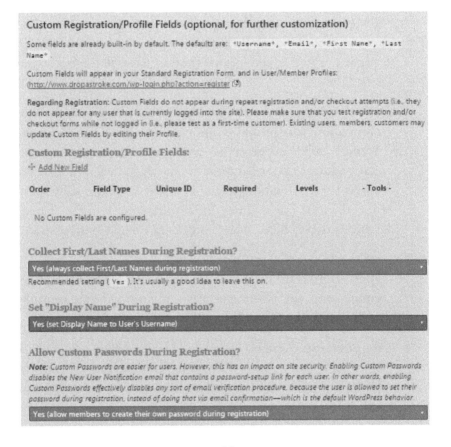

11. **Login Welcome Page:** In an earlier step, we created two pages. Here, we'll want to select the "Members" page. This lets the S2Member plugin know that your Members page is protected from non-members and will also redirect members to this page once they log in. If your Members page isn't an option, you might have left it in draft status (which I did myself while setting up this very tutorial). It's an easy fix — just go back and make sure both pages are published.

12. **Membership Options Page:** This is where you select the other page, "Subscribe." This page will display your payment buttons. Leave the other option at the default Yes.

13. **Member Profile Modifications:** You can leave this page at the default settings for now.

14. **URL Shortening Service Preference:** Leave this at the default settings.

15. **Make sure you click on "Save All Changes."**

You now have the basic foundation of your membership site! Let's set up the payment options next so we can make some money.

Setting up PayPal

S2Member allows full integration with PayPal accounts to ensure that everything is seamless. There are just a few settings you will need to configure in S2Member and your PayPal account.

Under your S2Member tab, click on the "PayPal Options" button.

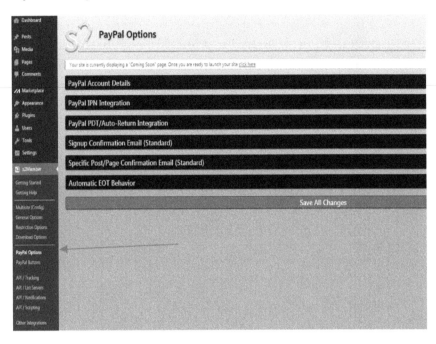

Once you click the PayPal Options button, you will see the six tabs listed above to configure your settings.

1. **PayPal Account Details:** You will need to fill out all of the required fields.

   a. **Your PayPal Merchant ID:** You will need to upgrade to a PayPal business account if you don't have one. Then you can find your merchant ID under My Profile, then My Business Info. Your merchant ID will be listed under your name, email, address, etc.

   b. **Your PayPal Email Address:** The email address where you get PayPal emails.

   c. **Your PayPal API Username:** In your PayPal account, go to Profile > My Selling Tools. There you will see API Access. If you just set up your account, click Update. Then scroll down to the NVP/SOAP API Integration section and select Request API Credentials. Make sure Request API Signature is selected and hit Agree and Submit. There's your Username, Password, and Signature.

d. **Your PayPal API Password:** See step C above.

e. **Your PayPal API Signature:** See step C above.

f. **Leave everything else at the default settings.**

2. **PayPal IPN Integration:** This step provides the instructions you need to follow. You will need to log in to your PayPal account and enable your IPN.

3. **PayPal PDT/Auto-Return Integration:** This tab also provides its own instructions for you.

4. **Signup Confirmation Email (Standard):** This tab is prefilled for you. It's for editing the confirmation email that is sent to new members who complete payment. Feel free to customize as you see fit.

5. **Specific Post/Page Confirmation Email (Standard):** This one is prefilled for you as well, but can be customized to your preferences. This is for when visitors pay to access a specific content piece on your site. They don't actually become a member.

6. **Automatic EOT Behavior:** This is prefilled also and the default settings are fine. This tab is designed to tell the S2Member plugin to cancel a member's account if they cancel their subscription payment, have a dispute, or request a refund. The only part you may want to update is the "Refunds/Partial Refunds/Reversals (trigger Immediate EOT)?" section to the below option.

Refunds/Partial Refunds/Reversals (trigger Immediate EOT)?

Full Refunds, Reversals (these ALWAYS trigger an Immediate EOT action)

And there you have it! You have just created a fully functioning membership site! Those are all of the required fields to get your site functioning properly.

There are some other tabs we didn't cover, but those are for extra features that you don't need until you get a more advanced membership site.

Payment Buttons

These are the instructions for setting up the button visitors will click on in order to make a payment and become members. Without it, you won't make any money, so don't forget this step!

Go to S2Member tab and click on "PayPal Buttons."

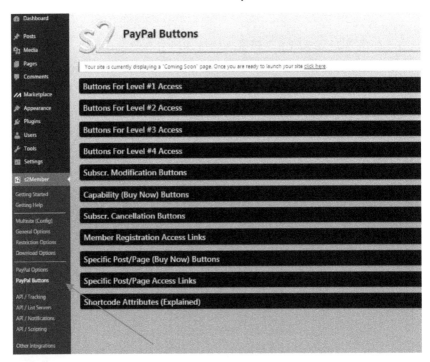

For ease of use on this example, we can assume that we will only have one level of membership. We will charge $25 per month, but for members who commit to a longer timeframe (six months, one year, two years, etc.), we want to offer a discount. Let's use $125 for a six-month membership.

Click on the "Buttons For Level #1 Access" from the tabs listed above. Based on $25/month, our tab would look like this:

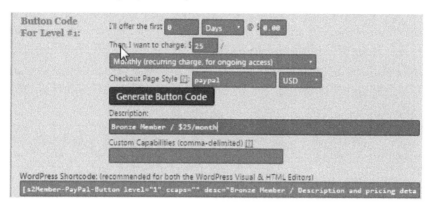

Once you type in $25, select Monthly (recurring charge, for ongoing access), and update your description field. Then click the "Generate Button Code" button. A code will automatically become highlighted, and all you have to do is copy that code and paste it directly onto the Subscribe page that you created earlier. Make sure you hit "Update" on the Pages tab so your changes are saved.

For your $125 six-month membership option, your tab would look like this:

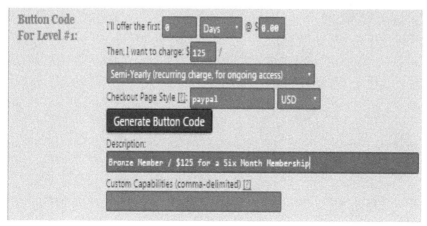

You can create any membership variation you want. From yearly to quarterly, even daily, the options you have to choose from are endless.

You are probably wondering what the Level #2, Level #3, and Level #4 tabs are for. In our example, we set up $25/month as our Level #1 membership. Once we get a few members, and the content on the site becomes really valuable, you could create another page on the site for more great material and charge more to gain access to that page. That is where you would use the Level #2 tab and create a PayPal button for $50/month. The tab setup is exactly the same as Level #1, so you should easily be able to create that button using the same steps.

Level #1 members will only have access to Level #1 content, but Level #2 members would now have access to Level #1 and Level #2 content, and so on and so forth as you go up in levels.

How to Set Up the Members Only Content

We've got the site all set up, we've got payment buttons — now we need to set up the rules so that non-members don't have access to member-only pages. Since we've only set up Level #1 membership, we just need to assign "Require Level #1 (or higher)" to the content that we want for members only.

Go to your Pages and create a new page. I named mine Content for this example. On the right side of the page you will see the below S2Member box.

s2Member™   ▲

Page Level Restriction?

[▼]

* see: Restriction Options · Pages

Require Custom Capabilities?

[   ]

* see: API Scripting · Custom Capabilities

All you have to do is hit the drop down button and select "Require Level #1 (or higher)".

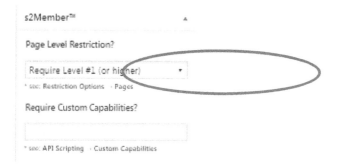

Once that is done, make sure to select "Update" or "Publish" to save your changes. This "Content" page is now only available to paying members. If visitors try to access the page, they will automatically be redirected by S2Member to the Subscribe page!

Getting Members

This is obviously the hardest part of the process. It only took an hour or so to set up our fully functioning site, so if that was all it took to have a six figure site, everyone would be doing it. The difficult part is finding individuals that are willing to pay your fee.

Trust

Trust is the biggest key when it comes to getting members. Your visitors have to trust you in order to send you money for a subscription. You can earn their trust in a few ways:

- Offer a Free Trial: Once they see how valuable the content on your site is, they will be compelled to join. This can really have an impact on your sign-up rate. People love to test things before buying.

- Offer a Free Membership Option: the key is to build trust over time. Once they see the site in action and understand that even the free option has solid content, they will be very curious to know just how great the paid content is.

- Offer a Free Membership on a Different Site in the Same Niche: This is a great way to build a membership base for future sites. If you can build, let's say, a 100-member free site about widgets, then create a paid site about those same widgets, you now have 100 members already interested in that paid site and who already trust you that will likely be eager to sign up. The trick is to offer value for free and then leverage the trust you earn by doing so.

Traffic

In order to build a big subscriber base, you have to drive traffic to your site. More specifically, you have to drive *targeted* traffic. If you have some money to spend on advertising, you can use Google Adwords. Take some time to define very niche-related, specific searches so that the people who do land on your site actually want to be there. Instead of using "golf" as one of your keywords, use "how to select the best golf shoes." Now the only visitors who will likely come across your page about golf shoes are people looking to buy golf shoes.

Before signing up for paid advertising like Google Adwords, it is imperative to test your landing page. Make sure it's as easy as possible for visitors to enter their email address so that you can build your mailing list. Offer them free value by saying something like, "This eBook is too valuable to hand out publicly — just enter your email address and I will send it to you privately."

You can also use SEO (Search Engine Optimization) to get your site ranked as highly as possible in Google search results. I can't possibly teach SEO here, but there are plenty of videos and tutorials on the web to help you learn. You can also pay someone on upwork.com or fiverr.com to optimize your site, which may be the preferred method if you don't want to dedicate hours to studying this practice.

Happy Members, Happy Life

If you want members to continually pay you month after month, you have to make sure they are getting their money's worth. They need current and valuable information. Here are some of the most common (and profitable) types of membership sites:

Software Subscriptions

This is arguably the most popular type of site. This gives paid members access to specific software. For example, JungleScout.com, which I mention in the Amazon FBA chapter, is a software subscription site. You pay a monthly or yearly fee and get to use their software.

Teaching

Offering advice, tips, or tutoring on a specific subject is another example. If you have a wealth of knowledge on a specific subject, you can consider creating one of these sites to share your knowledge and help others (like creating a course on "How To Create a Membership Site in One Hour" like I've just done for you here). If you don't know much about the subject of the site you created, you can even hire writers on upwork.com or fiverr.com to write content for you that you upload to your site.

These are just a few of the types of membership sites out there. The focus really comes down to giving your members great service. Always put yourself in their shoes. "Would I pay $25 a month for this?" "Can this content be found for free?"

How To Make $100,000 Per Year With a Membership Site

Solve your members' problems! This is the ultimate key to generating a very profitable site. Most of the searches that are typed into Google are by people looking for a solution or looking for help. Be that solution.

If you are really and truly solving problems for people, getting to six figures with your site shouldn't be that difficult. Here's an example.

Let's say you have a membership site that costs $20/month and 5% of the members cancel every month. If you are able to enroll 20 new members per month, by month 12, you will have approximately $3,600 in revenue from 180 members.

Using the numbers above, in 24 months, you would be very close to the six figure goal just from the monthly recurring membership dues. You could incorporate affiliate sales, advertising, etc. to produce even more income.

CHAPTER 7:

Blogging

Blogging is becoming one of the most popular strategies for generating online income. Everyone sees these success stories of bloggers who make six figures per month and think they can easily do it themselves. Just create a blog and then the money starts pouring in.

That's not how it works, unfortunately. Most blogs don't make any money for years and years. They have to be nurtured and cared for like a newborn. Creating a successful blog can take more time per week than a full-time job and that workload may last years, but once you get everything set up properly, it can become a gold mine that requires very little continuous effort.

In this chapter, I am going to go through the step-by-step process that extremely successful bloggers use to set up their blogs.

Why Should You Create Your Blog?

The key to any successful blog is being able to provide value to visitors. If you don't, it won't be successful. It's really that simple. What does value mean? Value means anything that helps visitors in any way, shape, or form.

You need to find a niche that you want to blog about. Maybe you've found a popular hobby, but when you click around on all the blogs about it, you don't really find anything useful. That can be a great niche to join. The key is to stand out and provide extremely valuable content — usually for free. Get used to giving away value for free, because it pays huge dividends later on.

So what will be the point of your blog? How will your blog benefit visitors? Can it give them great, ACTIONABLE advice or is it the same old garbage that everyone else is producing? A lot of times on blogs, you will find the exact same information posted over and over with different names and numbers, and none of it really gets into the details of doing something. Define the point of your site and get very detailed on the steps needed to get to the desired outcome.

If you overheard people talking about your blog on the street, what would you want them to say about it? Think about that as you post your content. Make sure your material gives visitors reasons to speak ecstatically about it. Imagine hearing someone saying they came across your blog and put your plan into action, and now their lives have changed. Does it get any better than that? Maybe your blog is about grooming golden retrievers. Make sure you deliver your explanation in full detail so that every visitor can go home and groom their golden and they will come out looking like show dogs.

Whatever the subject is, make sure it really and truly helps people that come across it. Solve people's problems.

How To Create a Blog

The first step to creating your blog is buying a domain name and arranging your hosting services. Just like creating a membership site, you can use the same services such as GoDaddy, BlueHost, HostGator, etc. Upon signup, you will need to fill out all the information and pick a plan. The one-year plan is a good place to start. I am going to be creating a golf-themed site, and I'll use www.dropastroke.com for my domain.

Installing WordPress

Once you've got your domain, hosting, and a website, you will need to log in to your account with your hosting provider. Then click on the option to install WordPress. Leave everything at their default settings for now. It is recommended that you deselect the recommended themes and plugins box as we will tackle that shortly. Click Complete and you have now installed WordPress! You will definitely want to write down the login and password information, as the passwords that they assign you are impossible to remember.

Once you log in to your site using the Admin Site URL and your login information, you will be presented with your WordPress screen.

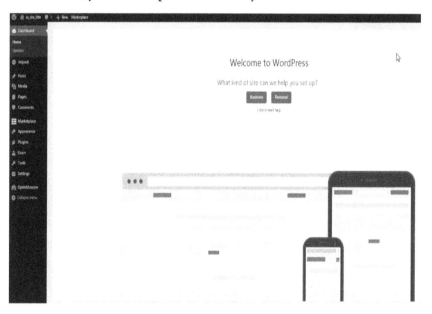

WordPress was created with the average person in mind. You don't have to be a techy computer person to figure this thing out.

Let's start by changing the name of our site to make it work with our domain. I will change mine to something golf related in this example, but feel free to use any name you want. Go to Settings > General and enter your site name in the field marked "Site Title." You can also update your Tagline, which will show up under your title when the site is live.

As you can see, I've updated my site title to "Golfing Secrets" and my tagline to "Where Golfers Go." Once you've made your changes, hit Save at the bottom of the screen. I hate the thought of losing any work I've done and having to redo it, so I save after pretty much every change I make. You never know when the power will go out, so save often.

Permalinks

Permalinks are the URLs of the content that you publish to your WordPress website. They are what people enter into their browser's address bar to view one of your pages, and they're also what search engines and other sites use to link to your website. This makes them extremely important for the searchability of your site.

To find your permalinks, go to Settings > Permalinks. Everything comes pre-populated, but you will want to make some changes.

Click on Custom Structure and copy/paste the following:

/%category%/%postname%/

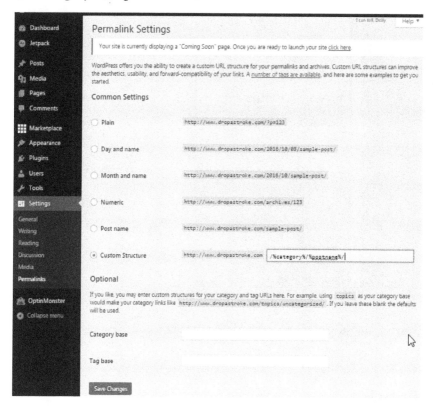

Picking a Theme

WordPress offers thousands of themes for you to choose from, both free and paid. Go to Appearance > Themes > WordPress.org Themes, and you will be presented with as many themes as you could want.

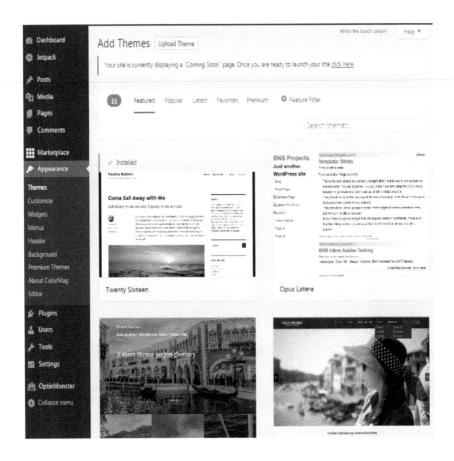

Once you find one you like, click "Install" and then "Activate." I have picked the theme "ColorMag" in my example. Once you've activated it, you are now free to write your first post!

Publishing a Post

Creating a post in WordPress is extremely easy. Just go to Posts > Add New. You will see a box that says, "Enter title here." This is obviously where you enter the title of your post. In this example, I will title my post "Golf 101."

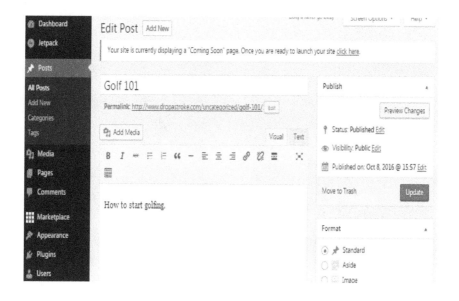

The box below that is where you will type the actual content of your post. Once you've finished writing your post, you are ready to publish. You will see a "Publish" button on the right side of the page. Click on that and you will see a green row pop up above your title box that says "Post Published." You just published your first post!

Contact Me

The main way visitors will get in contact with you is through a contact form. You can set this up yourself. Just go to Pages > Add New. Enter "Contact Me" in the Title box and then a short message in the description field. Something like, "If you have any questions or comments, please do not hesitate to email me. I will get back to you as soon as possible. Thank you!"

You now have a fully functioning page!

Before you make your site public, you will see a "Coming Soon" page when you visit the site. In the WordPress builder, you will see this bar on every page.

Your site is currently displaying a "Coming Soon" page. Once you are ready to launch your site click here.

Just click the "click here" text. It will then display a "Congratulations!" message and another "click here" button to view the site. Click on that and you will see your fully functioning blog site!

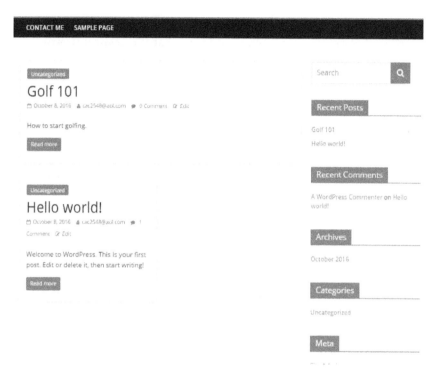

Of course, you now need to customize the site by adding photos, changing colors, and generally making it your own. Once you get the cosmetics set up the way you want, you're ready to start adding the valuable content.

Creating Valuable Content

This is the most important part of your blog — delivering valuable content.

Find out what people want and give it to them! Doesn't sound very difficult, does it? If the subject of your blog is something that you're an expert on, think about the common problems people have when they're just starting out. What do newbies ask you, the expert, for help on?

If you can't think of anywhere to start, or you aren't an expert, head over to your competitors' blogs and see what the common problems are in your niche. Read the posts of the other blogs, but more importantly, read the comments. This is where visitors themselves ask questions. Think of this as your own personal focus group for your niche, and better yet, it's free. What common questions do the visitors ask? What do they want more elaboration on?

Once you find the common problems, write them down. Try to come up with six or seven questions if you can. Then you can create six or seven pieces of content around those problems and provide the SOLUTION. Once you provide the answers, you will be seen as an authority in your space.

If you aren't a good writer or can't create content yourself, hire someone from fiverr.com or upwork.com. Give them the problems you found and the relevant research that answers those problems. They can put something together for you.

One final tip: make sure the content that you are creating is by far, hands down, the best content on that topic. Read other articles to see what they are missing, and make sure your own posts answer all the important questions that a reader would have.

Create a Logo and Brand

A logo helps people remember who you are and recognize when you post something. It will help them distinguish you from the competitors in your niche. It is extremely important to create a fantastic logo and a recognizable brand.

Think about some of the items that you buy at stores. The other day, I came across this popular water bottle that was priced quite a bit more than the others, but was still selling like hotcakes. This water bottle is used for hiking and camping, and it's geared toward outdoorsy men and women. I looked up their Amazon sales using Jungle Scout (naturally), and couldn't believe what I saw.

They were selling millions and millions of dollars per month of these bottles and cups! I guarantee you that their actual product isn't any better than something you can buy from China for a few bucks, but they are outselling all of their competitors by leaps and bounds. Why? Because they have established their BRAND. Their logo is recognizable and people want to be able to say they own something with that logo on it. That's the power of branding, and you can use it for yourself.

Once people routinely come to your blog for answers and begin referring their friends to it, your brand is already growing. You have helped your visitors, and they now view you as an authority in that niche as a result. Don't let that go to waste.

How To Monetize Your Blog

Once you get great content posted on your blog and start getting some traffic, it's time to start trying to monetize that site. Let's discuss a few of the most common and effective monetization strategies.

Make it a Membership Site

Your blog is a resource for information. Visitors come to your page for the fantastic content you've created for your particular niche. It's only a natural extension to create some very premium level content that users will need to pay to access. You can create a single page on your site where only paid subscribers have access.

If you have established yourself as an authority and gained the trust of your subscribers, you should be able to convert a very high percentage of them to paying subscribers. Create content they can't live without. Make the resources on your site a must-have for your visitors' own personal businesses, and in most cases, they will have no problem paying for it.

Sell Information Products

By this time, your blog visitors already know, like, and trust you. You have provided them with the best content available on the web for your niche. They know everything you put out there is gold.

This is where you have the opportunity to start charging for some of your content. You may think this will be uncomfortable after you've been giving it away for free, but it won't be. These customers love everything you've given them, and they trust you. If you've done things correctly, you may even get some responses like, "It's about time you started charging for this content, it's too valuable for you to give away!" or "I feel like I've been stealing from you this whole time. I have no problem paying for this new product to make up for the free content I've been getting."

You can also create an eBook or training course on the subject and post it to your site for sale. You can also post your product on Amazon, Udemy, Clickbank, etc. for extra revenue, but your subscribers already know you and your value, so you will likely have better success with them.

Coaching/Personal Consulting

This idea isn't a passive income strategy, but it's often the most lucrative for those who implement it. You can charge much higher prices for personal coaching than you can for an online course. I've seen some of the gurus on the web offering their personal consulting or mentoring for $25,000+, and they have people signing up without batting an eye.

Especially once you're established as an expert and have real-life successes of your own that you share with your subscribers, people will pay small fortunes to get one-on-one time with you.

Remember, many of the subscribers to your site and buyers of your products don't actually do anything with the wealth of information you give them. That's why this option is so lucrative — it means people don't even have to sort through the information you've gathered in your products, because they can just hire you directly.

Physical Products

You have been solving your subscribers' problems for a while now. Then, you realize you can have some software developed that will solve it automatically. Then you sell access to that software on a monthly basis.

Adding a monthly recurring subscription for access to a problem-solving software, on top of a monthly membership fee, can exponentially increase your revenues.

You can even find products to sell from your blog. If your blog is about dog grooming, maybe you can have customized grooming brushes for sale on your site. Just get it made, ship it to Amazon, post it for sale on Amazon, and include a link from your site to the product. Once you sign up with Amazon FBA, Amazon will take care of the rest.

Affiliates

People buy a product through a link that you had on your site, and you earn money from each sale. While it sounds almost too easy, it really shouldn't be the bread and butter of your focus. If you're going to go this route, you should only promote products that you use personally and that help your customers get where they want to go. The product you're promoting should provide a solution to a problem that relates to your niche.

Creating your own products should always be your first option (the margins are much higher), but affiliates are a good follow-up.

Sell Your Site

Let's say you've built up a great blog with a large audience and lots of traffic. Now, you can sell it. In fact, people make a living buying blogs, revamping them, and then selling them. They do this over and over. We will cover this strategy in its own chapter later on.

The Six Figure Blog

YOU CAN'T MAKE $100,000 PER YEAR BLOGGING.

"OMG, what did he just say?" Yes, I said it. I know your heart just broke, but let me explain. It's impossible to make money just by blogging. Sitting at your computer and writing an article doesn't make you any money, does it? Does money start spitting out of your disc drive? If so, please email me and let me know which computer you use because I need to get one.

For the rest of us, we don't make money just by creating great content. The key to making money with your blog is to use it as a funnel. You use your blog as a medium to send traffic to your products.

The majority of bloggers all make the same mistake. They create their blog, create a ton of content that they give away, build up traffic to their blog, post a few affiliate links or ads, and then cross their fingers and toes that the money comes pouring in.

Yes, this strategy can work, and sometimes it does work. You can even make six figures, in theory. But if you combine that method with sending your traffic to your own offers, you can double, triple, or even quadruple the profit from your current traffic. Think of your blog like an ecommerce site — you want to drive traffic to your site so that they buy your products. You should treat your blog much the same way.

In one example, Yaro Starak (a blogging expert who I spotlight below), mentioned he generates on average $20,000 - $70,000 per month with his blog. $20,000 - $30,000 is the normal income with his standard membership site, affiliate links, etc. But his income gets to the $50,000 - $70,000 range when he launches new products and drives his current traffic/email lists to that product. That's the power of doing more than just blogging with links and advertising.

In another example I found online, a blogger made almost $22,000 in April 2016 alone. He is making a fortune with his blog, but guess what? Only around $10,000 of that was from advertising and affiliate commissions. Of that $10K, 40% of it came from sending his affiliate offers to his mailing list, and 60% came from advertising only. Since most bloggers don't have mailing lists, you could say that only $6,000 of that $22,000 came from actually blogging.

The rest, over $12,000 per month, was made from selling his own products. This is a truly powerful way to expand your blog without having to expand your current traffic or subscribers.

Basically, this guy has taken his $6,000/month blogging site and created a $22,000 online business with it.

Expert Spotlight

Yaro Starak, the founder of www.entrepreneurs-journey.com, makes a full-time living (the site has generated more than $2 million for him) with his blog about living the laptop lifestyle.

His first experience online was when he was in school. He was a big Magic: The Gathering player and absolutely loved the game, so he created a site around it. This is the perfect example of going niche around something you're passionate about.

After he graduated from university, Yaro created another site that was centered on connecting editors with students. He noticed that a lot of non-native speaking students who were studying at American universities were struggling with writing academic English. He was able to create a full-time income from that site because he connected people with a problem to people who can solve that problem.

In 2004, Yaro was told that he should create a blog around his editing site in order to drive more traffic to it. He created his blog, and for three months wrote about proofreading and editing for his blog. He realized that he really enjoyed the writing, and he ended up writing more about the business side of his blog. This led him to create another site (www.entrepreneurs-journey.com), on which he focused solely on the business side of blogging and how it works.

In the span of roughly two years, he started generating $5,000 - $10,000 per month from advertising alone using affiliate links, banner ads, and his mailing list.

Yaro kept hearing other successful bloggers say over and over that he needed to sell his own products. He decided to do just that and launched his first product later that year, which was a membership site. He was able to get around 400 subscribers at $29/month. That in itself is over $100,000 per year!

Yaro suggests that you should start out selling products and services and not focus on marketing, as it's hard to generate enough traffic to meet your financial goals through advertising. "Your conversion rate on affiliate sells will be much, much lower than the conversion rate of your own products to your own audience," Yaro explained.

The target he sets for his students is 10-20 new email subscribers per day. That way, at the end of a year, you have a nice email list of a few thousand subscribers. That's all you need to generate $100,000 per year. People opt in to your email list because they like you and want what you have to offer. You only need to get 100 of your subscribers to spend $1,000 over the course of an entire year to hit $100,000.

One of his main suggestions is to be very clear about who you want to target and who you want to help. Give people very specific information that helps solve their particular problem. Have a big point of differentiation with your content or products that separates you from the competition.

In short — be better than everyone else. Have better content, better headlines, better sales pages, and you'll see better results.

CHAPTER 8:

Authority Sites

What is an Authority Site?

An authority site is a website that gains readers' trust because of the high-quality content that it offers and the great experience that it delivers. Another way to put it is this — an authority site is a website that individuals in a particular niche are happy to have landed on, because it delivers great niche-related content and they enjoy their experience. The website users are happy to sign up and engage with the site on a consistent basis.

The key to building a great authority site is to solve people's problems. Give them a reason to come to your site. This goes back to having very detailed keywords in your page, so that when a visitor searches for "how to groom a golden retriever," they are guided to your page because you are the niche expert at grooming golden retrievers. Once you're able to help the website user with grooming their golden, most of them will continue to read more of your site.

Because of the value you provided to them, the visitor will have no issue signing up for your mailing list, or referring their friends to your page. You will be able to form an online relationship with these people. They need to know, like, and trust you.

After you have helped them once and they've signed up for your mailing list, you can further your relationship with the customer by making yourself real to them. Send helpful, niche-related emails to your list, but also tell them about yourself. Explain why you started the site and what first brought you into the niche.

There are a few main criteria for delivering a top-notch authority site:

- The site is focused only on one distinct niche.

- The site really and truly helps people who are reading the content.

- The site is not all about promoting affiliates and making a quick buck.

- The site mainly focuses on building the readers' trust and engagement, and fosters user interaction.

- The owner actually engages the users in the comments, social media, etc.

If you are an expert on a particular hobby or type of work, creating an authority site can be extremely profitable. Over time, authority sites can consistently deliver five, six, or even seven figure returns if you can really deliver fantastic content and offer meaningful engagement with your users.

Jon Gilham, the owner of www.authoritywebsiteincome.com (yes, his site is an authority site about authority sites) and business partner in multiple other online businesses, has recently been able to quit his day job as an engineer and rely solely on online income to support his family. He has been able to generate $10,000 - $16,000 per month with his sites. He defines an authority site as a site that adds value. It's not repeating what's already been talked about, but it's a site that provides fresh material and solves people's problems.

It's much easier to do this if you have experts to write the content. Expert advice is one way of adding value, but there are plenty of other ways that your website can become an authority site. One such way is including a tool that helps people solve a specific problem. If there's a site that talks about that problem and then provides a simple online calculator or downloadable program that can help people solve that problem, then that site, in Jon's mind, is an authority site.

Jon went on to explain how he started out with authority websites. While he was still in college studying to be an engineer, he got a job at a small startup. One of the tasks he was assigned as a co-op was to build a website. He had no idea how to do that, but he did some research and discovered oDesk.com, which has since become Upwork.com. Jon was struck by the opportunity to outsource projects like website building for what appeared to be remarkably cheap rates and get really decent work done. He kept pulling that thread and began to think, "If I can get them to build a website for the company, there must be a way to get them to build websites relatively cheap that make money." That's where the snowball started to roll for him, and he focused on figuring out systems and procedures to go as systematically as possible in building up websites that generated ad value and income.

How To Identify a Market

Identifying your authority website market is really the same process that you can use for your eBooks, Amazon products, membership sites, etc. The key is NICHE.

You want to pick a solid, broad market. But wait, didn't I just say niche in the sentence before that? Yes, I did. (Good catch.) First, you identify a good market — let's say golf, for example. Then you identify your sub-niche from that. Let's say your site will be targeted to left-handed female golfers. Your sub-niche should be the main topic of your site.

Making sure your sub-niche market has items to sell is critically important. One of the big aspects to monetizing your site will be through affiliate marketing, so make sure your sub-niche market has products for you to sell to your audience.

The next step is keyword research. Make sure your sub-niche has some low-competition keywords that can generate traffic. You can look up keywords with Google Adwords, like we talked about a few chapters back.

Jon's advice on keywords is that you've got to look at the keyword research from a market standpoint. Don't think, "Here's a specific keyword that I'm building the site around." Instead, take a wider perspective from a market research approach and think, "Here's a specific problem this authority site is going to help people solve," and then, "Here is the total set of keywords that I'm going to go after."

Within that set of keywords, what are the metrics that John looks for? High volume, low competition. Of course that's the ideal situation, but more specifically, he uses a website tool called Long Tail Pro and looks for competition value under 30 and for the cost of articles created to be relatively low. He doesn't mind going after keywords that have low volume.

Essentially, this analysis lets Jon see that there are enough keywords in that space that he doesn't need to be dependent on only his two keywords he's trying to rank for. Otherwise, "if I don't rank for these, I'm in trouble," Jon explained. He wants to see, in this niche market, that there are a ton of low competition keywords for which he can create targeted content.

How To Get Great Content

Writing Your Own

Jon is a huge Wayne Gretzky fan, and one of his favorite quotes from hockey is, "Go where the puck is going, not where it is." In his experience, he has seen that Google rewards the best content with higher rankings, so his sites may as well have the best content. According to Jon, everything else comes easier after that. Having the best content isn't enough all on its own, but you may as well start with the best content. That's where he made the decision that if he was going to create a site, it was going to have the best content in that space.

If you're the expert in this particular space, then great content should be very easy for you to create. Just write down or record all of your expertise and knowledge, package it neatly, and give it to your audience. But if you aren't the expert, things are different.

Outsourcing

Jon explained how he is able to make his authority sites even more passive by outsourcing a lot of the content creation. All of his sites are run by a team, with the exception of his personal site, www.authoritywebsiteincome.com, which is run exclusively by him. He only invests two to six hours a week, on average, in his main site.

All of his other sites are run completely by outsourcers. All of the outsourcers on his team are found on www.upwork.com, and he uses that site for everything from writing to day-to-day activities of the sites.

For his writers, he makes sure they are native English speakers and sends them all a test assignment, and based on that, he decides who to keep to deliver content for his site. For the test assignment, Jon simply sends the writers an instruction document, some details on what the article should be about, and some standard operating procedure on how to get the article created.

One of Jon's tips when communicating with his writers is to ask them to imagine that a family member has contacted them and asked a question. That puts the writer in the right frame of mind to go out and create the most useful, actionable article possible. The writing should essentially say, "Based on my research, here's what I found. I hope this helps."

Tools

Jon's first successful site was based around providing a downloadable spreadsheet to help with some financial calculations. He then offered it as a downloadable tool, and then included some content around that. He was able to sell some products and advertising off the back of that site and that traffic, but people were mostly coming and getting value out of the downloadable spreadsheet.

What's an example of a problem that can be solved with a tool on your website? Let's take real estate mortgages. If you can create a tool that helps filter out mortgage companies with great rates or ones that meet certain criteria, you can then include that on your mortgage-related niche site for people to use.

Whatever your problem is that you're solving for your niche, create an easy tool or calculator to address an aspect of that problem.

How To Monetize Your Site

Direct Leads

Let's say there's an insurance broker that wants customers, and Jon has built an authority site around helping new dads understand insurance. Then he generates a page that says, "Here's all the information you need to ask your insurance broker when you're a new dad to make sure your family's protected. And here is a link to get details to get contacted by someone in that industry."

Now Jon has a list of every dad interested in insurance who has signed up for that site. He can sell that list to insurance brokers who will pay big bucks to have access to such highly targeted traffic.

Affiliates

Jon suggests that the best way to build your authority site is make it completely free in the beginning. It's focused around a problem, and you're giving your visitors as much of the solution as you can through information.

Then the next logical step is for them to go and purchase whatever they need to complete that solution. For example, if your visitor is looking for a mortgage and is doing research about that topic, your authority site adds value to the conversation. From there, it's a logical step to say to your visitors, "here's your option A, option B, and option C – and when they take one of those options, you're getting an affiliate commission.

Expert Tips

Jon provided some great tips on being able to create a six figure authority site. You must have reasonably high standards in terms of maintaining the quality, along with a systematic approach.

When most people fail, it's because they think they have a great idea, work at it for three months, don't see success after three months because it takes a long time to get the organic rankings up, and then jump to a different project.

To combat this, Jon suggests putting a system in place so that even when the natural human response of "this project's not that interesting to me because it's not so shiny and new" kicks in, the system keeps running without your active involvement. That way, a month later, you can come back to see that the site is starting to get some traction. You'll most likely find yourself energized about it and ready to jump back in.

Jon suggests that you find a site that you want to emulate, so you have a role model as you're building up your own site. If you can visualize what the end product is and the amount of effort it's going to take, you're not going to get as discouraged in the process.

Now that you have a great authority site, how can you quit your day job? Jon provided the mental process he went through. For him, it was an eight-year journey to get there. He went through his most critical steps before making that decision.

First, set goals. Determine what numbers your business has to hit in order for you to be able to rely fully on that income. Second, define the risks that are associated with each of the businesses you have. Jon explained that he thought of his business as an income stool — if any one of the legs got chopped off, could the stool still stand? This kind of thinking helped ensure that he had some diversification of income and that he was protected from any black swan event that could jeopardize what he had built.

CHAPTER 9:

Digital Real Estate

How to Make Money Flipping Websites

The World Wide Web offers a multitude of ways for inventive entrepreneurs to make a profit. One of the easiest and most effective ways to do this is with website investing. There are three key ways to making money with websites: parking, flipping, and developing websites. You can start making a profit relatively quickly if you have a knack for the process. Let's take a look at those options in more detail.

Domain name parking:
In this method, you register a domain name, even if you don't intend to use it. Then you simply hold on to the domain name until you find someone who wants to purchase it, and sell it to them for more than you paid.

Website flipping:
In this method, you purchase a domain name and begin developing the site. Then, once the site has been somewhat developed, you sell it for a profit.

Website development:
In this method, you purchase the domain name, fully establish and develop the website, and then profit from the website itself.

Of these methods, domain name parking represents the smallest investment as well as the smallest potential returns in most cases. Using a website that you have developed is likely to provide the biggest profits, but this can be a slow process and it may be quite a while until you see any profit at all. Flipping a website is a medium of the two ends of the spectrum — it can return fairly impressive profits, particularly if you have experience with website development, and it doesn't take nearly as long as making money off of a website you own yourself.

You don't have to pick a single one of these methods and stick to it; try a combination, and don't be afraid to adjust your plan as you go along and find what works for you.

Regardless of what option you try first, the basic tenets of good websites are always the same: you want a simple but highly memorable domain name, solid keywords, and valuable content that would make a visitor want to spend time engaging with your site.

This chapter will teach you how to dive into each of these methods of profiting from website investment.

Domain Name Parking

The cheapest and easiest form of website investing is domain name parking. All it takes to get started with this method is the cost of buying a domain name — usually only a few dollars. Parking a domain name means that you own the right to the domain name and no one else can use it. If you've thought of an amazing website name, you can purchase the domain name before someone else gets it. The website will then display a "Coming Soon..." or "Under Construction" message to its visitors. You can let it stay that way as long as you like. Your domain registration is good for a year, and you can always renew it after the initial year expires.

If you decide to start developing your website, you'll need to purchase hosting (which is a separate fee from the domain name registration). Once a website is hosted, it is no longer considered a parked website.

Another option is to use a purchased domain as a redirection page to an established website. Say you own ExcellentWebsite.com. It's not a bad idea to purchase ExcellentWebsite.net as well — that way, you can set up ExcellentWebsite.net to direct visitors to the correct site in case people enter an incorrect URL. It also prevents competitors or lookalike companies from getting their hands on a domain name that can be confused with your own.

How do you make money off of a parked domain name? In short, you don't have to do anything — you just hold on to the registration rights until someone comes along who really, really wants to use your amazing website name, but they can't, because you already own it. Then you sell it to them for more than you paid for it, making a neat profit with very little effort. This practice was very common back in the early days of the dot-com era, but some savvy entrepreneurs are still making money this way. The trick is focusing on keywords and niche topics that a business is likely to want.

The Real Estate Analogy

It may help to think about domain name parking in terms of physical real estate. Imagine this — there's a big land lot for sale out in the middle of a rural area, and it's extremely cheap because there's nothing on it. No buildings, no foundations, nothing — just grass. But a few miles up the road, a huge shopping mall is about to open for business. Most likely, if that development spreads, this lot is going to be worth considerably more than it is right now in a few years when demand spikes. That means that when the area is no longer rural but a bustling commercial center, people will be willing to pay far more for it than you did when it was in the middle of nowhere. Since you bought it while it was cheap, you can resell it at a comfortable profit margin, simply because you were thinking ahead about what people will want.

That's more or less the same principle that applies to domain name parking. You don't have to put in a lot of money, because the domain isn't worth a lot right now — but if you make a good choice, it will be worth a lot to someone else down the line.

How to Buy a Domain Name That's Worth More Than It Costs

The idea behind domain name parking is that someone will eventually be willing to pay more for the domain than what you paid for it. Here are some questions to keep in mind when finding a domain name to invest in.

-Is parking the most valuable use of this domain name? Could you make a larger profit by actually hosting and developing a website? (More on this later.)

-Who would want to use this domain name? What makes it valuable? Is it similar to another website or does it have a desirable keyword combination? Something else?

-What keywords and catch phrases would be attractive to someone developing in a website in a certain niche? How can I incorporate that in a domain name?

-Do I have a way to market this domain name? Do I have access to people interested in the niche that the domain name relates to?

-Is now the best time to sell this domain name? If this is a developing niche, can I hold on to it and sell it for a higher profit in the future?

Domain name parking is simple and requires a very small initial investment — but it's not the only way to make money from websites, and it may not be the best method for you. Once you own a domain name, you can also think about website flipping.

How to Flip a Website

Website flipping is a more advanced, and potentially far more lucrative, method of website investment. The first step is the same — purchasing the domain name. After that, you'll actually host the domain name and develop it to create a functional website.

To put it in real estate terms, website flipping is essentially the same as house flipping. You find a property that's not in good shape, purchase it for a low price, fix it up to increase its value, and then sell it for a profit. With websites, you can either purchase a brand-new domain name and build a website from scratch, or purchase an existing website and make improvements to raise its value.

There are plenty of options whether you decide to create a new website from the ground up to sell it, or to find established fixer-upper websites and revamp them. In the early days of the Internet, it was easier to build a new website — but now that nearly every business has a website, there are a huge number of sub-par websites already in existence that could be improved for a profit.

Website flipping is more specialized than domain name parking, and you will need some specific skills to get involved in this aspect of website investing — namely, you'll need to know how to create fantastic websites that draw in traffic and provide value to a business who would want to buy it from you.

When Store-Bought Is Better Than Homemade

When deciding whether to make a new website or just upgrade an old one, there are some important factors to consider. For one thing, an existing website will come with an existing audience. That can save you a huge amount of time, and it may mean that you can greatly increase the value of the website almost immediately by simply amping up search engine optimization.

Along with a built-in audience, a website that's been around for a while will likely also have a comfortable network of inbound links, even if it's not a high-traffic website. An established website will also be indexed by search engines, which makes a huge difference in achieving high search result rankings and bringing in traffic. New sites will have to contend with the Google sandbox effect — which is essentially a temporary measure that keeps young websites from getting into the top slots of search results rankings. It can be hugely detrimental to your SEO efforts on a new site — but an existing page won't have to worry about that.

Buying An Established Website

There are several ways that you can make money off of an existing website that you purchase. One way is to find a website that is in the same niche as your primary business and is already receiving high volume of traffic. These visitors are already looking for the product or service you sell — so if you purchase a website that is getting a lot of this targeted traffic, you can redirect all those prospects to your own website. This is an easy way to funnel potential customers directly to your site. Of course, you'll need to make sure that the website you buy is pulling enough visitors, and the right kind of visitors, to make the investment worth it.

The other option is to buy a website simply to flip it and sell it. This can be a risky strategy. You'll need to carefully assess how much work the site really needs to become valuable, and the amount of time and money you'll need to invest before you see a profit. Not only that, but you'll also need to assess whether there will be a market for your website after you flip it. You can build the best website in the whole world for underwater basket weaving — but if no one is buying into the underwater basket-weaving niche, you're not going to make any money.

A great place to start in website flipping is to look for an ecommerce website that is selling a product in a well-established market, or a market that is just starting to gain ground. Remember, you're not looking for a great website — you're looking for one with plenty of room for improvement. If a website is already optimized, there's no point in flipping it.

Here are the key things that you'll need to know before you start flipping your first website:

-Find a website that has lots of room for growth, as well as a good market to sell it in once you've improved it.

-Get moving fast — hopefully you've already scoped out ways to rapidly improve functionality and profitability in multiple aspects of the website. You should see a measurable increase in sales, ideally in the double digits, so that you know your changes have been successful.

-Once the website is optimized, sell it quickly before your changes become outdated. You want to get the website sold before the market is oversaturated with businesses selling the same product that your site does.

Keep in mind that flipping websites is far from a guaranteed moneymaker. The Internet is an incredibly fast-paced and competitive marketplace, so you need to be quick on your feet and have a good eye for opportunity to get far with this strategy. Website flipping is best suited for people who already have experience in developing successful, profitable websites.

During my interview with Greg Elfrink of Empire Flippers (www.empireflippers.com), he mentioned a strategy surrounding flipping websites. He said he has a friend who will simply buy websites, spent just a few hours optimizing it by installing a simple plugin and rearranging the ad blocks. In one example, his friend purchased a website that was earning $1,200 a month. He spent a total of 10 hours over the next two or three months optimizing the ad blocks using a simple plugin. He was able to increase the website's income to $2,100 per month. Since websites are currently selling, on average, at a 23-24 multiple of monthly profit, he bought the site for $28,800 and, in just a few months, has increased the value of the site to $50,400. He can now almost double his money, not to mention the monthly income he generated along the way.

Developing Your Own Website

So far, we've covered domain name parking and website flipping. The third strategy is developing a website to profit from the site itself. Like flipping, you can choose to do this by creating a brand-new website or by improving upon an existing one. In most cases, it will be easier to upgrade an established site than to make a new one from scratch, so we'll start with that.

Think back to our real estate analogy. When you want to make money off of a property, you don't just buy the first one you see. You look for a house that has massive potential for value and is located in an area with growth, a property that has a low purchase price and a wide margin for profit. These are all the same qualities that you're looking for in a website.

How to Know A Website Is the One

There are a lot of websites out there. When choosing one to buy, here are some key ideas to keep in mind to avoid a costly mistake.

1. Take Advantage of Traffic on Established Sites

It takes time and effort to build up an audience, and websites that already have an audience are valuable — especially if they have an audience that's looking for the product you sell with your primary business. For this angle, consider these questions before making a website purchase:

- Does this website focus on the same niche that I'm interested in?

- Is this website drawing in traffic? Is it quality traffic, i.e., visitors that are actually looking for the product that I'm selling?
- Are there other problems with the website that might get in the way of making a profit?

2. Make Money From Ad Revenue

Instead of funneling visitors to your business's webpage, you can also make money directly from a purchased webpage with ad revenue. The ideal website for this method is one that has good content, but needs some SEO tweaks to build more traffic. That way, you can increase revenue with a few easy fixes.

Tailor both the ads and the content to a consistent audience, make all the necessary fixes to improve search rankings, and you can easily convert an under-performing website into a source of revenue.

3. Tap Into an Existing Community

This is one of the most lucrative things that a website can offer to a business owner or entrepreneur. Let's say that your primary business sells gardening tools. What you need to do is figure out how to reach the people who want to purchase gardening tools.

Now let's say that you find a website that's an extensive, established community of gardeners and all manner of plant-growing enthusiasts. No one is making any money here — yet. But this is a prime opportunity to monetize an existing community, because it provides you with access to the people who are interested in your niche.

There are a couple key aspects to finding the right community to reach into: First, the community must align with your niche, or provide some way for you to make a profit — if not directly with product sales, then with AdSense or something similar. Second, look for a community where the growth has outpaced the owner's ability to pay for bandwidth. Their forums or message boards may be so successful that the owner can no longer afford to host them — this is the perfect opportunity for you. Last, and most obviously, the owner has to be willing to sell. Get in touch with them and offer to purchase the website. Particularly if the owner isn't able to manage the website, you can most likely get a good price on it.

4. Pick the Next Big Thing

If you think you know what the next huge sensation is going to be, one strategy is to look for websites that have built up around that niche, and buy them before they can reach their full potential. A website that features a prominent keyword can provide a huge profit margin, if you buy it while it's still cheap and then have it ready for when that niche reaches its peak. Think about things like 3D printing, virtual/augmented reality, driverless cars, or other up-and-coming technology.

5. Buy Out the Competition

This is classic business strategy applied to the virtual world. If you have a business in a particular niche, but you have a certain competitor that's taking away your customers, one simple way to get on top is to buy out the competing website. Then, you can merge their website with yours and reap the benefits of the additional traffic and sales.

Of course, it might not be all that easy to get your competitors to agree to sell. You'll have to do some negotiating, so know what you're willing to give up. Even if it means sharing the profits, hopefully you can strike up a deal that's mutually beneficial to both parties.

If you go this route, keep these things in mind:
- Look for websites that are in your niche and directly compete with you for customers. Contact them to see if they're willing to sell.
- After they agree to sell, the work isn't done — you'll then need to incorporate both websites (or as many as you have

involved) into a single business.

- Typically, this scenario only works in well-established industries. In fledgling industries, there's often more effective ways to gain an edge over your competitors than buying them outright.

- You'll be incorporating this business into your own, so be sure that it's compatible and will complement your existing setup.

What's In A (Domain) Name

This is a similar situation to domain name parking, except in this case, you're the buyer, not the seller. It may be worth it to purchase a website solely so that you can have the domain name that goes with it, even if you intend to totally revamp the site itself.

The current owner of the website may not be willing to part with it easily, so you'll have to decide how much the name is worth to you. If it's a niche-specific, keyword-rich domain name that could mean a lot to the success of your business, don't be afraid to invest in it. After all, the whole principle of domain names is that they're extremely important to a company's online presence.

Finding and Buying the Right Website

No matter what strategy you're trying, you'll need to get started by purchasing a website or domain name. There are a couple of ways to go about this. Buying a domain name is fairly straightforward — just visit your preferred domain service (GoDaddy, Wix, HostGator, etc.), search for your domain and, assuming it's available, make the purchase. In most cases, for $10 or less, the domain name will be all yours for the next 12 months.

If you're planning to flip a website or develop one of your own, you don't want just the domain name, but also the website itself (the pages, content, framework, etc.). You can try your luck on "trading sites," which are websites for selling websites. However, these sites tend to be flooded with people looking to buy, which drives prices up. There's nothing wrong with trading sites — but there might be much better deals elsewhere, so investigate other options before you commit.

Do Your Homework

As with most important purchases, it's not a great idea to jump on the first website you see and pull out your wallet. Here are some tips on getting a great website for a great price:

- Make use of Google and Yahoo. Search for industries or niches you're familiar with and get ready to sift through a lot of search results.
- If a site is huge and obviously successful, don't bother with it — the owners probably won't be willing to sell, or if they are, they'll be looking for an exorbitant price.
- Don't be afraid to dig deep. The websites on the first two or three pages of search results could cost you six-figure sums to buy out, so you'll have to hunt around a little more for websites with lots of potential and more reasonable prices.
- Look for websites with a single webmaster, who may have been spent years curating content but never monetized the site. Remember that you're looking for a website that's decently ranked, but *not* one that's already been maxed out to its full potential, so find one with plenty for you to fix.

Purchasing a website is just like any other investment. There are risks and payoffs, and the best way to minimize risk and maximize payoff is to do your research. Be thorough and deliberate about your search, and eventually you'll find a website that's just what you need.

Making the Purchase

When you think you've found the website of your dreams, make sure you take a closer look at these aspects before you commit:

- Observe the website in its natural habitat for a few days. Watch for forum activity, blog posts, updates to the home page, or anything else that shows the activity level of the website or its community.
- If you can, try to dig back into website's history and see what changes it has undergone in the past.
- See if you can find out whether the website has established back links, and if so how many and where they're located.
- Assess whether the structure and design of the website is effective. This isn't asking if you *like* the website's structure and design — just if they're working efficiently.
- Determine how well the site has implemented search engine optimization and keywords. Remember, you're looking for a site that has plenty of room for growth. Do you see places where you could easily improve SEO and increase traffic?

This information will not only help you decide if this is the website for you, you'll also be better informed when you contact the website owner. You can do this by going through the website's contact form, if it has one. If they don't, try WhoIs.com to get the webmaster's contact information.

Keep in mind that even if you find the world's most perfect website, the owner has to be willing to sell it to you for it to do you any good. Buying a website from a hobbyist will typically be much easier, and cheaper, than buying one from a business owner. Regardless, you probably don't want to start by announcing your intent to buy the website. There's more information you need to determine if the website is really a good investment, and you need the owner's cooperation to find that out.

You'll need to delve into the website's facts and figures to see if there's anything under the hood you should be concerned about before you buy. Owners may not be willing to part with this information right away, so be polite and friendly when asking questions.

These are the key things that you'll want to find out from the website owner:

-Traffic statistics
-Costs
-Revenues
-Challenges or issues with the website
-How long it has been around

Assuming that the webmaster gives you all the information you need and there's no major red flags, you can proceed with your pitch about why they should sell to you. Think carefully about how you approach this conversation and emphasize that you want to invest and improve the website.

Once you've gotten the webmaster interested in a sale, you can move on to the transaction itself.

Finalizing the Sale

There are several very important steps to purchasing a website. Here they are:

1. After researching the value and negotiating with the website owner, agree on a price.

2. Transfer the domain to your name. Be sure to change the business name or incorporation information as well, if needed.

3. Transfer the website hosting to your name.

4. The website may use other design or analytics software. If this is the case, the software license also needs to be transferred to your name so that you can continue to use it. You'll need to contact the software company to make the change request.

5. Like any property sale, you want a contract that specifies the details of the transaction. For smaller websites, you can probably get away with a template contract. If it's a major transaction, it may be in your best interest to have an attorney oversee a custom contract. Typically, the contract will include a clause that formally ends the previous owner's access to the site, as well as a restriction that the previous owner will not start a competitor website for a certain amount of time after the sale. All parties involved will need to sign the contract.

6. Find out about all the email lists associated with the website. Download these lists and make sure you have access to them away from the website, in case the data is cleared out during the switch. Email lists are one of the most valuable assets that a website has to offer, and you do not want to lose it.

7. Make sure to get contact information for any editors, designers, or programmers working on the website in case you need to make arrangements with them in the future.

8. Don't leave anything to chance, and don't trust the website owner to take care of things on their end. Follow up on everything that you can follow up on to ensure you won't hit any unexpected snags in the future.

Create Your Own Site to Sell

Purchasing an established website to make a few simple tweaks isn't the only way to make a profit. There's another option — developing your own website from the ground up. This is much more difficult than buying an established site, and Empire Flippers strongly recommends buying established sites to start out. Whether you're making a website from scratch or just doing a major overhaul, here are the key aspects you'll need to keep in mind.

Choosing A Terrific Domain Name

Domain names are an extremely important aspect of your business. Choose carefully; this is going to be the very first impression that visitors get of your website, so you want it to be a good one. Remember these tips for choosing a stellar domain name:

-Less is much, much more. The ideal domain name is just one or two words in length. Three can work, as long as the overall name is still memorable and catchy.

-Get a jump start on SEO by looking for opportunities to incorporate a niche-specific keyword into your domain name.

-The more meanings your domain name has, the bigger the market of potential buyers if you sell the domain down the line. A broad, versatile domain name offers higher resale value than an overly specific one.

-Avoid easily misspelled words in your domain name. Domain parkers will snap up similar-sounding websites to make money off of visitors trying to reach your website.

After you have a great domain name in mind, visit Name.com, GoDaddy.com, or NameCheap.com to register it.

Finding A Website Host

Once you have your domain name, the next thing you need is somewhere to host it. A hosting provider essentially rents out space on their server so that your website has somewhere to store all the data that you'll be putting on it. Try to find a hosting provider that offers reseller hosting plans. Think of this kind of like subletting — you can offer a customer a place to host their own content via your site and earn a profit by doing so. Bluehost.com, GoDaddy.com, and HostGator.com are good places to start looking for this feature.

Content is King

Content provides value to customers and improves search engine rankings. If you're not much of a writer, not to worry — here are some other options for getting content on your site besides writing it yourself.

Resell Content: This is another kind of ready-made content for purchase, but unlike PLR, you can't modify or resell the text in any way.

Commission New Content: Hiring a writer to produce new content is the best option. A writer will create content that is tailored specifically to your site, and you'll own the full copyright for the text. It will be entirely unique, which is the best kind of content to boost your search engine rankings. You can easily find writers on upwork.com and fiverr.com.

After you've got your initial content up on the site, continue tweaking for higher SEO rankings and more traffic. Whether you're planning to sell the website or keep it for yourself, you want it to be as profitable as it can be.

SEO and Keywords

Hopefully, if you're undertaking the venture of investing in websites, you're already familiar with the basic practices of implementing keywords for search engine optimization. If not, you'll definitely want to brush up as you start to refine the content on your website so that you can build up traffic and earn money with your website.

Decide how broad or "pointed" you want your keywords to be by defining your target audience. Do you want to target a very small, specific niche, or a wider audience? Keep in mind that it's easier to resell a website with broad appeal than one with a narrow focus.

If you haven't already, learn to love Google Adwords; it's designed to help you find the best keywords for your niche, which is extremely helpful for improving search engine rankings as well as AdSense campaigns.

Indexing

Indexing is a critical step for a successful website. Essentially, having your website indexed means that search engines are able to include it in their search results. For most businesses, it will be extremely difficult, if not impossible, to build up a solid audience without strong search results rankings, so you definitely want to make indexing a priority.

Unfortunately, indexing doesn't happen immediately. It will take some time for new sites to be indexed and start to climb through the ranks. There are, however, some steps that you can take to speed up the process.

All Press Releases Are Good Press

Press releases are an excellent way to get your site indexed. There are a multitude of services online that will allow you to place a press release to announce your website's launch. Be sure to include a URL in the release that links directly to your website — this will help get your site indexed and improve traffic. As a bonus, if you decide to sell the website in the future, you'll be able to show a potential buyer that you've already placed press releases for the site. This will help prove that you've been taking steps to build an effective, profitable website.

Get Found on Craigslist

Craigslist is a Google algorithm's dream: it's a website full of unique, constantly updated content, two aspects that search engine rankings reward highly. There's no cost for posting on Craigslist, so you can take advantage of Google's favoritism by creating an ad for your website.

Simply go into the Services Offered category and write a post detailing why your website is valuable to visitors (be sure to include your URL!). Do this for one or two cities and you're all set — any more and you risk being flagged by either Craigslist or Google as spam. But even a post or two will likely get your site indexed faster and on the way to topping the search results.

Sitemaps

Google offers another great tool to get your sites indexed faster. The Google SiteMap website provides software that will crawl through your website and essentially produce an organized list of every distinct URL that is included in it. This list, called a site map, can be submitted to search engines (all of them — not just Google) which will allow for much faster indexing and more efficient search results, since the search engine already knows about every page of your site and can direct visitors accordingly.

Indexing by Hand

Instead of waiting for the search engines to find you, you can bring your website straight to them by submitting your URL directly. Just go to the main page of the search engine and submit the URL of your website. This doesn't just apply to Google — you can also do it for Yahoo!, Bing, MSN, and others.

Taking Your Website to Market

If you've gotten this far, congratulations! Getting to the point of selling your website means you've done lots of research, chosen a niche, purchased a site or domain, and built a profitable website. That's no easy task. Luckily, this is the part where your hard work pays off.

Many people want to buy websites that are already successful. It saves them all the time and effort that goes in before a website turns a profit: designing, curating content, researching niches, and optimizing for search results — basically, all the things you've already done. When you've got a successful website that you're ready to sell, here's what you need to know.

Selling Your Site

Flippa.com

Flippa.com is currently the biggest and most popular place to buy or sell websites. You can even buy domains and apps, too. There are over 700,000 buyers and sellers on the site, according to its page, so there should always be an interested buyer for your niche site.

Empireflippers.com

Empire Flippers can also sell your site for you and they are the best in the business at what they do. Check them out at www.empireflippers.com.

Here are some great tips, provided by Flippa, to get your website sold for the highest price. Please note these tips are not specific to Flippa. These should be used on any site you use to sell your website.

Be Descriptive: Many unsuccessful auctions on Flippa have very little information in the description. From a buyer's perspective, if you're not willing to go into some detail about your site it's usually a bad sign. You need to have a high-level summary or overview at the top of the auction copy, and then use the rest of the description to dig into the details. Use headers to break up the blocks of text and point directly to the various sections in your auction copy.

Attention to Detail: While most buyers will be forgiving of a misspelling or two, you'll want to make sure that your data and statistics are tight across the board. It's a red flag if you're mentioning 7,435 visits per month and then saying 9,305 visits further down the auction copy. If English isn't your native language, pay someone to write your copy in a way that you just plug in the numbers from the site you're selling.

Transparency as a Differentiator: People tend to buy from people they know, like, and trust. It may be hard to build rapport in your auction content, but consider linking out to your social profiles and show you're a "real person." Buyers find it scary bidding on auctions that are anonymous, so I always put a link to my blog, LinkedIn profile, etc. This shows buyers that I'm not hiding and it communicates confidence that I'm someone they can work with, should there be any problems. Since many sellers prefer to remain anonymous, being transparent is a great way for your site to stand out.

Stop Overselling: Buyers do have a "If it's too good to be true…" philosophy, so stating that your $800 site could, "easily be earning $1,000 per month in a couple of weeks" isn't going to help. (If it were true, why don't YOU do it and sell for more?) It's okay to paint a positive picture, but you're much better off taking a matter-of-fact approach. Don't focus on figures when it comes to explaining the site's potential. Overemphasizing figures might also low-ball the value that a prospective buyer sees in your site (e.g saying your site has the potential to earn $1,000 per month, when the buyer sees an opportunity for $5,000 per month).

Build History and Trust: If you want to sell sites on a regular basis, it's important to build up trust and a solid reputation. Just like auctions that have viewers or watchers, Flippa also has a

"Watched Seller" feature. This feature automatically sends out emails to watchers when a seller they follow lists a new site for sale. Additionally, we implement an "undersell, over-deliver" policy with all of our buyers which has kept our feedback 100% positive and has led to glowing reviews. Even if you only sell larger sites once every one to two years, build your selling history with smaller sales to get top dollar on your next major sale.

Pricing Strategy: It may sound crazy, but we price all our auctions at $1 with no reserve. This guarantees that the website will sell and have an excellent chance of reaching the first page of Flippa's "Most Active" section. It also narrows our focus. Now that we know the site is definitely going to sell, our job becomes clearer – do everything to get as many views as possible! This strategy has been instrumental to getting top dollar for each and every auction we've listed. "If you're selling something of value, let the market determine the price."

If you can't stomach the idea of no reserve, list your auction at $1 and place a reserve that's the absolute minimum you expect. While it's not as attractive, you can still get enough bids to feature in "Most Active." By the last 24 hours, you'll hopefully have passed the reserve. There's nothing that says you have to give away the reserve price even when potential buyers ask. Giving it away gets may get you an early bid right at the reserve price, but you will lose you all those smaller lower-end bids that are required to feature in "Most Active."

Bidding Strategy: We start with manually accepting bids at the beginning of an auction and switch to automatic during the end. The reason is simple – we want to maximize the number of bids to ensure getting featured in "Most Active." For example, I may launch an auction and get a $500 bid. Instead of accepting that bid, I'll sleep on it, wake up the next day, and see that I have four additional bids under $500. I can now accept all the bids, including the $500 one. That's a total of five bids instead of one, which helps my positioning.

Be aware of savvy buyers. They want as few people as possible checking out your auction so they can avoid a bidding war. They may offer their best bid early with the hope that you'll accept right away. That higher price discourages other bidders and helps the high-bidder keep the auction out of "Most Active."

Don't Sell Short During "The Dip": You'll get an initial burst of views when your auction goes live, and then things will slow down. Way down. The middle of your auction is the dark period where there won't be nearly as many views. Savvy buyers know this and will try to reach out and get you to short-sell your site to them directly. If they make an offer you're happy with, feel free to take it — but we've found that these offers are generally much lower than the price we ultimately get if we keep the auction going.

Promote Outside Of Flippa: While Flippa will do everything they can to sell your auction successfully, it doesn't hurt to help them out! When you're starting your auction at $1 (and with no reserve) your job is clear – get as many targeted visitors to your auction as possible.

Look at where you hang out online and see if you can use your authority in that space to drive interest to your auction. If you're selling a site in the health niche and are a regular member in a health forum, consider linking to your auction in your signature. Search for related posts in that forum and add value to the conversation. This will naturally lead to more visits to your auction. Don't be spammy; a soft approach is best. Include your link as a regular part of your conversation and you'll do just fine.

Auction Comments: You'll notice that live auctions have a visible count on the number of comments made. This is another form of social proof you can use to get more click-throughs to your auction, so we use comments to provide updates regarding earnings, traffic, etc. We also respond to every comment we receive on the auction, effectively doubling the amount of comments. Again, there's no reason to be spammy here. A few updates and responding to each comment will ensure your auction is interesting and lets prospective buyers know that you're on the ball.

Six Figure Websites

Investing in websites can be a highly profitable strategy for Internet marketers. If you're familiar with the basics of website design, SEO, and online marketing, you're already equipped to start making money with this method.

The most effective use of this strategy, however, isn't with a one-time flip-and-sell. To make the most of the potential for website investing, you can work on five or 10 websites at a time, or even more. You can optimize each of these websites and let their value build as they age, then sell them on a rolling basis to maximize your earnings.

Whether you choose to start with domain name parking, website flipping, or website development, there's ample opportunity to combine and customize these options to find the perfect method that works for you. Think of these strategies as tools, and with them, you can build your own highly successful online business.

We'll conclude with some final helpful tips:

> - As with anything else, the best way to learn is by doing. Jump in and try out these strategies — the faster you do that, the sooner you'll see your first profits.

> - Get involved with the community of Internet marketers who are employing similar methods as you. Connect with other professionals through blogs and forums to hear about the latest news, tools, and strategies for success.

> - Keep an eye on your competition; they're a valuable learning resource. Learn from their successes as well as their mistakes.

- Have an agile, flexible approach to website investing. Make sure you're constantly evaluating your practices so that you can correct weaknesses and build on your strengths.

- There's no upper limit to website investing. Your earning potential is essentially unlimited, so keep challenging yourself to find new ways to grow and expand your business — you might be surprised how far you can take it.

According to Empireflippers.com, websites are currently selling at around 23-24 times profit. That means you only need to build your site up enough to generate $5,000/month in profit in order to sell it for a six figure payday. Follow the steps in this chapter, in the membership site chapter, the authority site chapter, or the blogging chapter and you could see a six figure payday sooner than you think!

Greg, the content manager at Empire Flippers, provided some great tips for getting a $100,000 website:

"Do really good keyword research. Really focus on keywords that are very uncompetitive, and one way you can do that is you can install the MozBar plugin and look at other sites with a similar DA – that's domain authority – as your site, and then plug that site into a tool like Ahrefs. If your DA is 18 and you find another website with a DA 18 in your niche, plug that website into Ahrefs and see what are they ranking for on the first page of Google. If they're ranking for it, there's a good chance you can rank for it and produce better content than those people. Also, definitely invest in some social media channels, because that'll help grow virally and help your website increase quicker.

As far as really quick, if you have the capital, I would do Amazon FBA. Amazon has an amazing amount of traffic. It takes 3-4 months, probably, before your listing will really go live, because you have to research a good product and then get that product, test it, make sure it's good, and then ship the actual product to the Amazon fulfillment place before your listing even goes live. But then once it goes live, it can be very easy to manage. Many people manage these Amazon FBA businesses by spending just 2-4 hours a week on them, if that sometimes. Just making sure they don't run out of inventory. So if someone wants to – not "get rich quick" or anything, but wants to see profit fast, and they have the capital to invest, then that's probably the best place for them.

One thing I would say, in my opinion – and of course, I work for a brokerage, so maybe I'm biased – I think buying a website is actually a lot easier than building one from scratch. Especially if you're new and you don't have a lot of resources available to you yet.

For example, we had this guy who bought an AdSense website from us that was earning $1,200 a month, and he bought it from us and in 2 or 3 months, he spent a total of maybe 10 hours on it over those 2 or 3 months, but he installed just a simple plugin. All he did was rearrange where the ad blocks go and decide which is the best position for the ad blocks. Because of that, it increased his website's income to $2,000 or $2,100 a month, so almost double what it was earning just 3 months before. And a few months later, he could sell that site for almost double what he bought it for, all just from those 10 hours of work. Plus he was getting the revenue throughout that whole process.

Versus someone building a site from scratch, SEO takes so long to write nowadays, you probably won't see a dime for the first 6 months of a content site because it takes time. That 9 among 10 where you earn your first Amazon affiliate commission and you earn that $50 check, a lot of people are like "God, I spent 9 months doing this for this $50 check," but what they don't realize, they're just right around the corner for that site to start ballooning up and start growing somewhere possibly very big.

Again, if you don't want to wait, buying a website is going to be a lot easier because you have a lot more to work with."

Case Study

The Amazon expert I mentioned previously, Will, has also had a few successful websites. And what does Will know about? What does he do? What is he passionate about? Amazon. So what do you think his site was about? Amazon.

Will found himself searching around the Amazon forums and realized the "experts" that were giving advice were individuals making $5,000 per month or less. While that is a very nice side income, Will was making 10 times that amount and thought he could provide much better advice. To give even more credibility to the site and cut out the fluff, he verified that each joiner was an actual seller — no "I'm going to ask a ton of stupid questions, but never actually sell anything" people.

He created a private forum for verified Amazon sellers called FBA Mastermind and charged $20 per month. The beauty of a private forum is your members produce all of your content. They ask and answer each other's questions with very little input needed from the owner. He ended up signing up about 150 members, enjoyed the $3,000 profit for six months or so, and then sold the site for $68,000! Better yet, he didn't spend a single dime on making the website. He traded some of his Amazon knowledge to website designers and they made   it   for   free!

CHAPTER 10:

Gold   and   Silver

Standard practice for gold and silver is buying bricks, bars, and coins and storing them until the value goes up. Especially in this cycle that we're in right now with money, people really want to own gold and silver to protect the value of their money. The problem with that strategy is that you can be sitting on gold and silver for 10, 15, or 20 years without it actually doing anything.

Minesh Bhindi, of www.goldandsilverforlife.com, has figured out a way to turn gold and silver into income-generating assets, much like real estate. What he does is help people use institutional strategies to actually make those gold and silver holdings start generating an income, so that while you're waiting for the value of gold and silver to go up, you're also making 1% to 2.2% a month in cash flow.

Think of it like a rental property. You own the asset, but you allow someone else to use it for a fixed fee every month. Ideally, this fee is higher than your monthly cost and you're able to pocket the profit. In this case, your rental property is gold and silver.

How It Works

Minesh and his team use ETFs and options to do just that. The ETFs are Exchange Traded Funds, and they work like this: a fund manager sets up a fund and all the capital in that fund is held in

155

physical gold and silver. The advantage in doing this is that you can use options on the market to generate cash flow. Now, most people will run from this prospect if they're not experienced investors, but options are just vehicles that were created by the very wealthy to allow people to speculate on the stock market.

The way Minesh and his team use options is the way that they're meant to be used, which is to provide an income, to allow other people to speculate and for the holder of the asset to generate an income from that asset. According to the Chicago Board of Options Exchange, 90% or 95% of options speculators lose money every single month. The problem with the investment education world is that 95% of investment education courses teach people to speculate with options. Minesh and his team do the complete opposite, and that's why they have a 92% independently verified success rate for their clients. Obviously, they don't have the promises that you're going to make 11%, 12%, 15% per month guarantees in inverted commerce that other people do, but again, this company has been running for six years now and they have clients in 40 countries and a 92% success rate — so the strategy works.

If you had 10 ounces of physical gold, you would have to convert that by bringing it back to cash and then purchasing the ETFs with that cash. You've got to be very careful as to which ones you use, simply because there are funds out there set up by people that either are being dishonest about the amount of gold that's held in that fund, or a lot of it's held in cash for a long time. Other funds are what's called leveraged ETFs, which you don't really want to use either. That basically means for every dollar that gold loses, the fund might move $2 or $3 in that same direction.

As far as the ETFs go, the only funds that you want to look at are GLD and SLZ, simply because they're the biggest and are set up by the biggest institutions around the world. GLD was backed by the World's Gold Council, founded by them, and is managed by some of the biggest authorities around the world. It was the fastest growing

ETF in history and has capital holdings at around $70 billion. These are not play funds; these are real funds.

The way it works is that you own stock, just like owning a property. Then you go and find a tenant for that property. The only difference is that in this scenario, the tenant gets the right to buy your property for a certain price by a certain date, which is typically a month away from today, for example. The "tenant" will pay you a premium for holding that price for a month. They make money if the stock shoots through the roof, which is what they think it's going to do. Minesh makes money if anything else happens. Typically, the rules make it so that the stock price going up at a certain point doesn't happen. That means that 95% of the time, Minesh and his team are making money simply because of the speculators losing out. The other 5% of the time, they're making money because the price at which they agreed to sell the property, so to speak, is higher than the price at which they purchased it.

For example, let's say an ounce of gold is $100. A speculator comes in, and the price of gold stock is sitting at $112. He thinks it's going to go to $119 or $120. The price goes up a little bit more to $114, so he'll think, "Okay, this is definitely going to happen." Now you, as an options trader, go in and sell what's called a call option at $115, which basically gives the speculator the right to buy that stock if the price goes above $115. What Minesh and his team do is they use their analysis tools to tell them what the probability really is of that stock going above $115.

Let's say the analysis finds that the probability of the stock price going any further past $114 and breaching $115 is low. At that point, Minesh and his team decide to give the speculator the contract.

Now what? Over the next month, more than likely from the probabilities determined by Minesh's analysis, is that the price is going to come down rather than go up. If the price comes down, you keep your premium of $2 or whatever the speculator has given you up for the right to do that. In his head, if he's giving you $2, at $115 his total cost is $117. If it goes to $120, he's made $3 profit. All he's given you is $2 to hold the stock for that month-long period. The speculator will be making a huge return if it works his way. More than likely, the price is going to come down and go back towards $100. At that point, you get to keep that $2 premium, and you get to do the same thing the next month.

How to Make $100,000 With Gold and Silver

Generating six figures with this strategy depends on a few things. Number one: it depends on how much capital you're starting with. The proven ROIs are 1%-2.2% per month with this program. People can reverse how much capital they're going to need to see if this makes sense for them.

Secondly, it depends on how fast they go through the program. Minesh's program is six hours long, but somebody might need to go through it three times. Minesh also offers weekly coaching calls for people to attend indefinitely. They have clients that joined in December of 2010 who are still attending those Q&A calls today, and they've never been charged again, even though the entry fee for the program has quadrupled.

If your goal was $100,000, you would need to have $1.2M - $2M worth of capital. By the way, that's without capital appreciation on gold and silver.

Basically, you can think of this process as a self-generated dividend. You acquire the gold and silver (stock) and you get monthly income from owning it (dividend payment). Just like owning dividend stocks, you also get the aspect of wealth generation, depending on how long you're going to be in the market. Some of Minesh's clients have $100,000 in gold and silver, and they're going to be making a ton of money not only from gold and silver going up, but also in the cash flow they're going to generate over the next five to 10 years that they're holding the investment for.

Key Takeaways

One of Minesh's big keys to success is, again, just get started. You have to do the doing in order to see how it really works. Theory doesn't make any money.

In one story he told, he realized why he didn't actually need to go to school for business after high school. When he was in high school, he had started a business. He was 16, speaking on stages on the weekends, making good money, and then going to school and listening to business studies teachers. There was one time where a project was to write a plan for a business project.

"I created this whole business plan on a business that was already running. So let me just put this into perspective. I was making more money than these teachers, at that age, and they were asking me to write a business plan about a business I would do, right? Just to set the pre-frame. So I wrote this business plan for a business that was already running (and making $15,000 per month!) and for the first review, the teacher looked at it, threw it back in my face and said, 'Who's going to buy anything from you online?' Then she went over to somebody else who created a business plan, with all due respect, out of her backside, which needed $300,000 of investment capital that she had no idea where to get from. It was a tuition center in the middle of some neighborhood. The reason why she was rewarded is because that business plan was believable. The work we do is not believable to most people."

Her business plan was "normal." It's so strange to most people that you can make money without a "real" job.

Trading Silver for Real Estate?

"I absolutely believe that every single person on Earth right now should figure out how to buy about $5,000 worth of silver." – Minesh Bhindi

Let's say you take Minesh's advice and buy that $5,000 worth of silver today. How can you generate $100,000 per year with that? In one article written by Jeff Clark, a Senior Precious Metals Analyst with goldsilver.com, he outlines exactly how owning a relatively small amount of silver today could potentially buy you a vacation house in the near future.

The formula is really pretty simple:

1. Buy enough silver today.
2. Watch real estate values decline.
3. Watch silver prices rise.
4. Sell your silver when the panic sets in and pick your house.

The pricing trends of silver and real estate tend to move in opposite directions — as the value of silver goes up, the value of real estate often goes downward. If you can work both of these trends to your advantage, you can buy the maximum amount of real estate for the minimum amount of silver. Based on the historical data, we may be headed right into a confluence of these two factors.

Real Estate

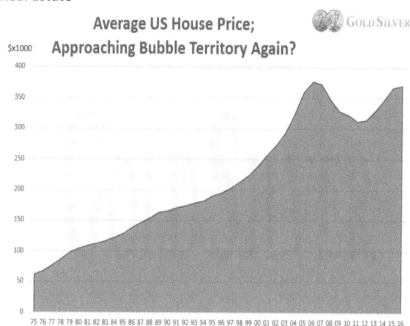

Average US House Price;   GOLD SILVER

$x1000   Approaching Bubble Territory Again?

Source: Federal Reserve Bank of St. Louis

The first of these trends to contend with is real estate. The average home price has spiked 18.5% between 2012 and 2016, a pace well above the standard rates of growth – except for one notable period: during the mid-2000s, leading up to the record home prices of 2006.

Real estate experts have reported that homes in the San Francisco area have been selling above asking price throughout 2016. That's an almost certain indicator that the bubble is growing again, and fast.

Sooner or later, increasing prices will bring rising interest rates. Higher interest rates in turn will bring falling demand, and with it, falling prices. This could come about in one of two ways — either the Fed will raise rates directly, or inflation will drive up interest rates within the next few years purely through market forces. If this corresponds with the crash that financial experts have foreseen in the stock market, the drop in real estate value could be even more dramatic.

Analysts project that interest rates are likely to stay stagnant for a few years yet, but if history teaches us anything, it's that there's only a matter of time until the bubble pops.

Gold and Silver

Across the board, industry experts agree that precious metals are now in a bull market. Typically, bull markets aren't as transitory in the gold and silver markets as they are in other sectors, often lasting two to three years at a time.

The upcoming rise in silver and gold prices is set to far exceed the standard cyclic boom. Considering the unprecedented surge of currency that's been put into circulation, the market will need to account for all the excess money that's been printed — and it very well could do so by creating an equally unprecedented surge in silver prices.

Historically, silver's growth outpaces gold's. Gold prices jumped an impressive 2,328% at the height of the precious metals surge in the 1970s — but silver positively skyrocketed to 3,105% at its record high. It's not impossible that silver will see similar growth during this cycle.

How   Silver   Can   Buy   Your   House

As you can imagine, if the silver market's peak lines up with the real estate market's valley, there are some truly phenomenal deals to be

Ounces of Silver to Buy a Median-Priced US Home

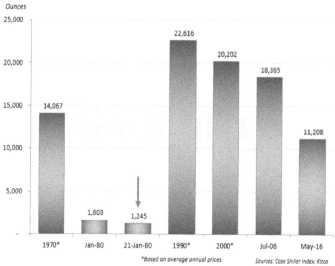

*Based on average annual prices   *Sources: Case Shiller Index; Kitco*

had by the smart investor.

This graph shows the number of ounces of silver needed to purchase a median-priced home in the United States. The lowest ratio occurred on January 21, 1980, when only 1,245 ounces of silver were needed to purchase an average house. That's when silver hit its all-time high of $50. For those who didn't manage to sell right at the peak, that month's average for silver was $38.80; investors who got that price for their silver needed 1,603 ounces to cover the cost of a house.

This ratio is even more impressive considering the real estate market at that time. Home values rose sharply throughout the 1970s, from a median price of $23,000 in 1970 to $62,200 in 1980. But despite the median price nearly tripling over the previous decade, the ratio fell precipitously when the silver frenzy hit full tilt. The lesson here is that real estate values don't necessarily need to fall to reach these record low ratios. A major spike in silver prices could be enough to create those ratios all on its own — and if the current predictions are correct, it's on track to do just that.

The same trend is proven again in the time after 1980. Even during the peak of the housing bubble in 2006, the ratio continued to decline because the rising silver prices were outpacing the median real estate value.

If the trends follow through the way they have in the past, the ratio could once again fall to a measly 1,245 ounces of silver to purchase a typical American house.

CHAPTER 11:

Dividend Investing

Dividend investing is an investment strategy that focuses on only buying stocks that pay a dividend. If a stock doesn't pay a dividend, you don't buy it. In case you don't know what a dividend is, a dividend is a sum of money paid regularly by a company to its shareholders out of its profits.

The best companies that you can look into for dividend investing are the "blue chip" dividend companies, which means they are well-established companies that are profitable and provide very well-known products and services. These types of blue chip companies will have a large market capitalization, which will help an investor filter out smaller and less established companies.

To find the ideal long-term, dividend-paying companies to invest in, check out the Dividend Aristocrat's list, which only lists the companies that have paid and grown their dividends annually for 25 years. Those companies are fantastic to set up a compound growth portfolio where you reinvest all of your dividends to produce more dividends.

Dividend Investing Metrics

In order to choose which companies to invest in from the Aristocrat's list, or any dividend-paying company for that matter, you should analyze them more closely on your own. Here are the

165

main factors that most investors use when analyzing their dividend stocks:

Dividend Yield

The dividend yield is the annual dividend divided by the price of the stock. If the company pays a $5 yearly dividend and the stock price is $100, then the yield would be 5% ($5/$100 = 0.05). The yield is how much money you will get back every year for owning your stock. It's typically best to stay in the range of 3% - 6% when picking your stocks. If they pay less than that, you won't be very satisfied with the return, and if they pay more than that, the company may not be able to support itself in the long term as they are paying out everything in dividends instead of focusing on growth.

Payout Ratio

The payout ratio is the percentage of a company's profits or income that it pays out in the form of dividends. A company that consistently pays out everything in dividends won't be able to grow the business, or the stock price for that matter. To calculate the payout ratio, you take the yearly dividend divided the company's stock price increase over the course of that year. For example, if a company paid out $15 in dividends this year and earned $20 per share, the payout ratio would be 75% ($15/$20 = 0.75). The best range here is probably from 30% to 75%, as that typically shows that the board of directors is serious about reinvesting profits to grow the company, but also wants to pay the shareholders.

Price-to-earnings (PE) Ratio

The PE ratio is simply the stock's price relative to its per-share earnings. If a company's stock price is at $20 and they earned $5 per share over the past four quarters, their PE ratio would be 4.0 ($20/$5 = 4). Basically, the PE ratio indicates the dollar amount an investor can expect to invest in order to get back a dollar of that company's earnings. It is best to look at stocks that trade at less than 20 times their earnings.

$100,000 Dividend Plan

Ultimately, the goal for most dividend investors will be to retire from the dividend payments and leave the investment principal intact. That way, you don't have to worry about cashing out any of your portfolio, and with dividend increases, you should be able to hedge against inflation. But our goal is to get to $100,000 per year in dividend payments as fast as possible, so let's see what it takes.

First, we have to start by figuring how much our dividend portfolio needs to be worth in order to generate $100,000 per year. I want this scenario to be extremely realistic, so let's use a conservative dividend yield of 3.5% (dividend yield is the annual dividend divided by the price of the shares). To get to the amount we need to generate six figures, we just take our goal of $100k divided by 3.5%.

$100,000/3.5% = $2,857,142.86

I know what you're thinking. How on earth could you possibly get your portfolio up to $2.8 million? Well, remember, there are 12 interviews in this book with actual, real-life passive income experts who have divulged all of their secrets on how they got to six figures. If you follow the tips in this book, it may not be as hard as you think.

Not only that, but the 3.5% is very conservative. Maybe you can achieve 4.5% dividend yield, which would cut your target by another $600k to $2,222,222.22. One thing you have to remember — this is by far the most passive of the passive income investing options out there, so it's only logical that it is typically the slowest process. But could you imagine getting $100,000 per year for literally doing nothing once you get your portfolio to the target? That would be incredible! Not only that, but your multimillion dollar portfolio value won't be affected whatsoever once you start cashing the dividend checks.

"The goal of retirement is to live off your assets — not on them." — Frank Eberhart

Now we have our target portfolio amount of $2.8M. Typically, dividend investing is for the very long term investor with decades of investing in front of them. For the next 35 years, if you can save $2,000 per month at 6%, you will theoretically hit your goal of $2.8M in portfolio value. Don't have $2,000 to invest each month? Use the strategies in this book! If you reinvested every dollar you made trying each of these strategies, you could knock this number out in half the time!

CHAPTER 12:
Royalty Companies

Savvy investors are always looking for ways to strengthen and diversify their portfolio. One undervalued but powerful way to do so is with royalty companies. These are companies that provide a financing mechanism for new mining operations in exchange for a percentage of profits or heavily discounted gold or silver.

Whether you're a novice in resource stock or a long-time expert looking to refine your investment strategies, royalty companies might be the ideal addition to your portfolio.

What Is A Royalty Company?

A royalty company is, in short, "a mine-financing entity that has sold shares to the public," according to John Doody, one of the world's leading experts on gold and silver. In an interview with Stansberry Research, Doody explained that these are businesses that essentially provide capital to mining companies, either in the exploratory phase or in the actual construction of new mines and processing plants. Royalty companies can be considered competitors with bank lenders and brokers with equity offerings, and miners often prefer to work with royalty companies over either of these other options.

169

How Do Investors Make Money with Royalty Companies?

There are two basic payment models for the way that investors make money with royalty companies. With the first model, the royalty company is financing an exploratory program before the mine actually goes into operation. They do this in exchange for receiving a royalty on any future sales that result from a discovery of gold or silver, typically between 1% and 5%. The amount needed to begin an exploratory program is not very high — often just a few million dollars — but the returns can be considerable. Some royalty companies may receive up to $50 million per year from a mine that they helped finance during their exploration program, even if the initial investment was 30 years ago.

The second model is focused on funding the actual mine construction instead of an exploration program. This phase is more expensive for the mining company, and represents a bigger investment for the royalty company. In return, the royalty company receives a "stream" — a royalty payment that's based on a specified number of ounces per year, or a fixed percentage of the ounces produced annually by the mine. With this model, the royalty company may be able to purchase gold at a 75% discount from the current spot price, if they supply enough capital to the miner upfront.

For mining companies, streams are the ideal financing method for a new operation. In his interview with Stansberry, Doody explained why this is: "If they borrow the money from a bank, they might have to hedge the production...or the bank might want more security of other mining assets, and so forth. If they sell more shares to finance the mine, it dilutes – and irritates – existing stockholders." On the other hand, royalty companies offer the mines an easier source of capital, and in return the royalty company benefits from the production of the mine.

170

Why Are Royalty Companies a Unique Opportunity for Investors?

Royalty companies offer a number of notable benefits to investors. One of the most important ones is that they're a terrific way to diversify. A standard mining company might own only one or two mines, which represents a substantial risk if one of those mines were to encounter setbacks or difficulty (which mines often do).

On the other hand, a mature royalty company is typically earning royalties from anywhere between 10-50 different mines. Even if one of those mines were to fail, the rest could make up the difference. This allows investors to take advantage of the lucrative precious metals market without the high degree of risk that comes with mining companies.

For example, Royal Gold is one of the largest royalty companies in the world. They have fewer than 24 employees, but the company has generated more than $300 million in sales over the last year! That's over $12.5 million in sales per employee. Where else can you find numbers like that?

Silver Wheaton, another large royalty company, employs 30 people at most, and yet it is able to generate around $500 million in revenue. That $16 million per employee! It's very possible that Silver Wheaton is the world's most profitable company from a revenue per employee standpoint.

Another key advantage that royalty companies have over mining companies is that a royalty company will not be responsible for capital cost overruns. Mines frequently go over budget during the initial phases of construction and operation, and mining companies often need to put up more money than they originally anticipate — but not the royalty companies. They simply make a one-time deal that secures a certain amount of the mine's profits, and they have no obligation to assist with budget overruns.

Additionally, royalty companies don't have any exposure to rises in the cost of production, and that's a significant factor in the gold and silver market. In the early 2000s, the average cost of gold production was approximately $200 per ounce. That average had climbed to $650 by 2012, and it's on track to rise even higher. Mining companies have to deal with these steeply rising production costs; royalty companies don't.

Besides all these benefits, probably the most important factor to an investor is that in most cases, royalty companies pay considerably higher dividends than mining companies. Because most of the royalty companies, even the major ones, have fewer than 20 employees, their overhead is typically very low, and that means a high profit margin. It's common for over 90% of royalty income to go into gross profits, which then becomes dividends for investors as well as financing for additional mining properties. That comes to about 20% of their royalty income being paid out as dividends, which is a much higher rate than you would see coming from a typical mining company.

Royalty Companies in Practice

One of the best examples of the potential of a royalty company is Royal Gold. This was a company that started quite small with just a few properties on its roster. One of those properties was Cortez, a mine in Nevada where gold was discovered. A company called Placer Dome developed the mine, while Royal Gold retained a royalty on the property. Cortez was eventually developed into an extremely successful mine that produced close to a million ounces of gold per year. The income from the royalty on Cortez allowed Royal Gold to acquire more properties to repeat the same process. Eventually it grew from its humble beginnings to a multi-billion dollar business.

For investors looking to take advantage of a company like Royal Gold, the basic guidelines are these: larger royalty companies typically trade around 20 royalties per share, meaning that a company with $2 in royalty income per share will be priced about 20 times that, or $40. The smaller royalty companies will have a trading multiple about half that much, typically around 10 times royalties per share.

Of course, that's an average, not a fixed amount. To make the most of your investment, buy from small companies that are trading around five times royalty income, and sell when they're trading close to 10 times or more royalty income. For big companies, buy when they're trading close to 15 times royalty income, and sell when they're trading at more than 25 times income. But buying and selling based on the company's trading multiple may not be the best option. In the long run, you may be better off buying and holding, depending on the company's pipeline of growth.

CHAPTER 13:
Other Passive Income Strategies

Create Software

Software can be an extremely lucrative source of passive income.

Just like anyone else, I'm assuming you have your fair share of problems. Write them down and brainstorm ways to solve them. You can't track which of your students has paid for their lessons? Create software that can track it for you! This is a real-life example from a case study in the "4 Hour Work Week" book by Tim Ferriss.

Brandon was a music teacher and couldn't keep track of which of his students had paid and which hadn't, so he decided to create a very simple application to help track the payments. Eventually this got a little more sophisticated and began generating $1,000 per month. Today, Brandon's software includes a full suite of offerings, as well as a DIY website element.

When he first reported on it to Tim in late 2011, it was already bring in $25,000 a month (90% of which was passive income!).

Don't know how to program software? I know I don't. Outsource it! Just like almost everything else in this book, it's extremely easy to find programmers online in places like www.upwork.com or www.fiverr.com. Any programmer worth their weight will be able to create basic software, and basic is all you need to start.

174

Armand Morin is another expert at creating software (check out www.armandmorin.com.) He finds a need in the market and then goes to his programmers on Upwork of Fiverr, tells them the specifics of the program that he wants created and gets people bidding on his job programmers on Upwork or Fiverr, tells them the specifics of the program that he wants created, and gets people bidding on his job.

"My customers started asking me, 'It would be great if someone could come up with a piece of software that could do this.' I searched the internet, I found a programmer – because I knew that's what I needed – and I described to them what I wanted. They went ahead and developed the software for me. And I called it E-book Generator, and I released that out to the public. That was my first time I ever did that, and I found it to be pretty easy. All I had to do, from that point on, was just produce the product that they wanted. Ask them and then produce it."

The average piece of software Armand develops costs him less than $300. Anytime that you would want an additional revenue stream, whether it be an extra $100 a month, an extra $200 a month, an extra $1,000, in some cases an extra $10,000 a month, all you have to do is simply create another product and solve another problem for somebody. And by solving that problem, people are going to want to buy that product, which means additional revenue streams for you.

Armand posts projects on Upwork, and all of his descriptions start the same way: "This is a very simple project for a programmer who knows what they are doing." Now, think about this. If the programmers come back and say, "Well, that's a real complicated project, I'm going to have to charge you a lot more money," what are they saying? They're saying they don't know what they're doing.

Once he has hired a programmer, Armand provides two precise statements that tell them what this project aims to do. He doesn't have a flow chart or a big diagram. Most of his projects are done between three to 10 days from the time they are posted.

REITs

REITs or Real Estate Investment Trusts are stock shares of companies that own real estate investments, most of which are commercial properties, in the United States and even globally.

This type of company was created in 1960 when Congress passed a law that REITs would not have to pay corporate income tax if they passed at least 90% of annual income on to shareholders as dividends. This created a huge tax advantage for REITs as real estate holding companies, and even non-real estate companies like McDonald's have considered forming an REIT to hold their land ownership.

Investors win because the mandate means higher cash payouts for REITs compared to most traditional stocks. The Vanguard REIT ETF (NYSE: VNQ) pays a dividend yield of 3.9% annually, nearly double the yield paid by companies in the S&P 500.

REITs can be far more passive than typical real estate investments. Unlike real estate rentals, your investment in REITs does not require around-the-clock management to fix broken water pipes and secure rental permits. Buying a few funds that hold shares of REITs can diversify your investment across different property types and geographically.

Conclusion

One of the main things that was highlighted by every expert I interviewed is to start. Plain and simple. 95% of people, even the ones that read every book out and attend every seminar out there, never actually get started. You can pay all sorts of money to learn the theories, but until you actually start trying things for yourself, you won't make any money. Theory doesn't pay.

Try SOMETHING today! There are 14 strategies listed in this book. Pick one and try it out. If you want to try Amazon, buy a cheap product TODAY and see if you can sell it. You will learn more from creating an account and doing the selling than you will from any book. Then, once you learn the process, the books and strategies you have read about will all make more sense.

If you want to try eBooks but don't think you're a good enough writer, research articles and send them to a writer on upwork.com or fiverr.com and get a book written for you. Use that same outsourcing site to have someone build you a website and then post your book. Do that TODAY.

Get on upwork.com and find a writer to write you a 40-page book on a topic using the Kindle Publishing chapter as your guide. In just a few days, you can have a book published!

Only YOU have the power to change your life. It starts today.

"Nothing will work unless you do." – Maya Angelou

If you enjoy learning about passive income in this book, a review would be MUCH appreciated! Leaving reviews is the best way to help your fellow readers differentiate good books from terrible ones so make sure to help out your fellow readers and passive income enthusiasts!

Make sure to check out my series titled 'Your Path to Success.' The first book in the series is titled Fail Your Way to Success and it highlights how great achievers view success and how they used failure to their benefit every single time. With failure they not only elevated themselves, they took humanity to greater heights with them.

About The Author

Author Chase Andrews devoted a year to discovering the secrets of passive income. His journey would take him on a global quest, travelling the world to meet and interview ordinary people who had "cracked" the *Passive Income Code*.

In 2013 Chase Andrews was an employee in an unfulfilling job at a consulting firm, until a chance encounter would change his life forever. Attending a business conference in Europe, he met the man who would later become his mentor and help him "crack" The Passive Income Code. Within a few short months Chase was benefitting from 8 sources of passive income and was able to quit his job. He now travels around the US, Australia, and Europe with his wife, teaching people how to escape the 9-to-5 and secure their financial future.

The strategies revealed in this book will forever change the way you approach 'earning money'. You will never need another job again. And in time, you will discover that earning passive income is easier than you ever thought possible!

Chase recently discovered his passion for helping others escape the confines of the office and get out and enjoy life, all while making a full time income. Head over to www.thepassiveincomemachine.com to learn more about Chase, passive income, and how to escape the rat race.

CPSIA information can be obtained
at www.ICGtesting.com
Printed in the USA
LVHW040950030119
602603LV00002B/88